The Tao of Golf

by

Leland T. Lewis

ISBN 0-88247-923-7

LC #92-54171

Published by
R&E Publishers
P.O. Box 2008
Saratoga, California 95070

Typesetting by
elletro Productions

Cover Art by
Judith Parkinson

Special Thanks and Gratitude

To my Pamela "Peach Blossom" Rose who encourages me to golf because it brings me joy. Constantly loves and supports me, and my visions. Is honest with me even at times when I think I don't want to hear it. Is an example of strength and courage beyond anyone else I have known in this lifetime, and brings the sweetness of a "Peach Blossom" into all that she does.

TABLE OF CONTENTS

Prologue

Certain rare golfers emanate a unique aura as they glide down the breath-takingly beautiful fairways that comprise the golf courses of the world. It is a particular presence that sets them apart. A mastery. If you are simply on the same golf course, you can sense their power, peace and confidence. These types are rare, and they carry that same power, peace and confidence throughout all aspects of their lives.

In the golfing world, they might be a touring pro, a teacher, or an amateur who plays purely for pleasure, without concern for reward or acknowledgement. But the one thing that all such players have in common is that at some level, they have pierced the inner understanding, appreciation and dominion regarding this ancient and elegant game of golf, and the even more ancient game of life. They have also obtained, in one degree or another, an advanced level of self mastery.

The presence that is emanated from such an illuminate is something that can be embodied and harnessed by anyone who carries within them the necessary desire, focus and receptivity. Unusual keys await you within the pages of this book. This is a golfing book unlike any other. It introduces you to a transcendental and mental mastery of the game, which is really too powerful for words, and must be experienced directly. However, the words within these pages can act as a pathway which will lead you to the doorway of profound personal transformation, using the wonderful and ancient game of golf as your vehicle. Once you are at that threshold, it is up to you. Will you enter?

Many recognize that golf is largely a mental game, and that mastery of the mind while golfing will lead to great results. It has also been scientifically postulated and widely accepted that human beings utilize only a small percentage of their mental capacity. A main focus within the following pages will be to illustrate how golf can be a quantum catalyst for transformation and growth of human potential. It will show how the performance upon the course will greatly improve as this transformation into a neo-awake state of awareness occurs. So in one sense, this is a book for transformation into mastery which uses the ideal setting of the golfing world as a perfect environment for rapid growth.

It is possible that as the reader you will be introduced to many things that you have never before considered, nor even heard about. If this is the case, good. Attribute it to the fact that one purpose of this book is to carry those who are ready into a brand new powerful and enlightened approach to the golf course, and life in general. It will introduce ways to access the major portion of the human mind and potential that lies dormant. If there are things within these pages that you do not understand, or are unable at this time to embrace, that is fine. Do not be concerned. Simply read on, and you will find much benefit. It is not the purpose of the following pages to convince anyone of the validity of the contents herein, nor to "convert" anyone to an alternative belief system. The contents herein are not a belief system, and it is recommended that the reader only embrace that which they experience to be true within their center. Those who are ready, will directly experience truth when they come upon it, within the very core of their being. No proof, nor justification is required, nor is it offered. It is all based upon direct experience. An experience which can become yours as you embody the knowledge, information and tools for transformation contained within.

Amateur — from Latin; amator, a lover.

Amare, to love. The amateur is one whose

participation is based upon pure love for the

activity.

This book is recommended to all golfers, whether they are beginning amateurs or successful touring pros. It is for any golfer who wishes to experience a profound uplevel with regard to their performance, ability, enjoyment of golf and life in general.

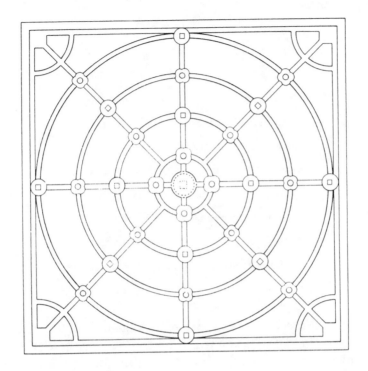

Align Center

"What is the Tao? If you can name it, that is not Tao."

This understanding is basic to the ancient Chinese philosophy of Lao Tsu, the venerable originator of the *Tao Teh Ching*. In its essence, the *Tao Teh Ching* is an ancient and time-honored philosophy centered around humanity's understanding of, and harmony with the laws of the universe.

Tao can be talked about, but not the eternal
Tao. Names can be named, but not the eternal
name. As the origin of heaven and earth, it is
nameless: As 'the mother' of all things, it is
nameable. So, as ever hidden, we should look
at its inner essence: As always manifest, we
should look at its outer aspects. These two
flow from the same source, though differently
named; and both are called mysterious. The
mystery of mysteries is the door of all essence.

-Tao Teh Ching

It will not be the purpose of this book to define the Tao (pronounced "Dow"), nor will it be the purpose to define the technically perfect golf swing. To define the Tao is to define the undefinable. And since various books successfully address the issue of the perfect golf swing, I will not seek to duplicate that effort here. It is the purpose of this book to chart new territory, and to offer you an essential edge relevant to an enlightened approach to golf and life in general. An edge designed to bring you greatly increased pleasure as you approach both life and golf from an entirely new, unique, and powerful point of view.

Truly, one purpose of this book is to describe the ancient universal Taoist knowledge in a way which will lead to insight as to the essential nature of the Tao (The Way) itself, using an ideal vehicle which is golf. Although the result of successfully utilizing Taoist understandings, (or Taoist magic as it was referred to by the ancients), in the game of golf, can inevitably lead to amazing results on the course for the golfer. This is somewhat paradoxical, because to understand the Tao as it relates to golf (or anything else), one must be devoid of ulterior motives or goals. One must also develop the ability to center one's attention into the Taoist point of most power, which is to be totally present with the entirety of your being and consciousness inside the present moment, *the Now*. It is from this perspective of "centered" attention that the power of the universe can be discovered and harnessed through the human vehicle. This universal energy can be used for any purpose which is in harmony with the natural and universal laws. But for the purpose here, we will illustrate how it can be used in golf.

Taoism is basic to the Chinese classics which define the ancient Oriental approach to such disciplines as: medicine, calligraphy, painting, flower arranging and archery as well as the Chinese martial arts such as Kung Fu, Tai Chi, Pa Kua (the eight trigrams within the arms), and Hsing-I, (the five elements beneath the feet). All of these forms are approached from the standpoint of understanding Tao. Also, since the Korean martial arts, such as Tai Kwan Do, and the Japanese martial arts, such as Karate, find their original inspiration from the ancient Chinese forms, they are also based in an understanding of Taoism. Because golf is a Western art form originating in Scotland, it of course does not find itself historically included among the ancient Chinese classics. However, golf is an ideal vehicle for bridging the wisdom and understandings of East and West in an experiential rather than theoretical manner.

Give up your little self, watch the whole universe. See, there's nothing binds you.

-*Zen Proverb*

Golf is an excellent vehicle for more fully understanding oneself, which is a basic purpose of Taoism. This is true for several reasons, but perhaps the most compelling is the fact that golf is, in many ways, a contest with oneself ... causing it to be an inner process rather than one which is first projected to the outside world, as would be the case if there were for example, a bodily opponent. The main opponent in golf is oneself. By obtaining a degree of self mastery while golfing, one becomes infinitely more prepared to master the various challenges of exterior conditions, such as the degree of difficulty of the golf course, or the weather conditions. Because golf is such an "inner game," it provides us with an ideal way to understand the laws of the universe and apply this powerful universal viewpoint in all aspects of life.

Finding the balance between Yin and Yang involves embracing the wholeness of who you are as a being. It places you at the center of the paradox of existence wherein apparent opposites harmonize.

Golf, when practiced from the Taoist perspective, becomes a mysterious experience in the quest for perfection. The highly aesthetic surroundings of serene green meadows, lakes, rolling hills, forests, and peaceful environment which comprise a golf course are an ideal setting, or laboratory, if you will, for understanding and harnessing the forces of the universe. Not only can the harnessing of this energy greatly enhance the golfing performance, it can also greatly benefit other areas in life, such as health, relationships, creativity, self-confidence, prosperity and happiness.

About Taoism

Taoism is experience beyond knowing through intellectual means, and cannot be interpreted or relayed even after the most unequivocal and incontestable experience. In a sense, one knows the Tao by "not knowing" the Tao. It is wholly beyond the conception of the mind. All that we can discuss here is the nature of the Tao as it is reflected within creation.

Taoism consists of three basic aspects which include *Yin, Yang* and *Tao*. The word Yin reflects the feminine principle of the universe, the attractive, the receptive, the creation, beauty, grace, omnipresence and the result of divine expression. The word Yang refers to the masculine principle of the universe, the active, creativity, momentum, power, expression of being, omnipotence and the origin of divine expression. The word Tao refers to the unseen aspect which is perceived as a perfect all-encompassing balance which contains the active Yang and the attractive Yin principles. It is within the Tao that the universal way is found. Perfect balance. Whereas an unbalanced Yang approach to life would be overextended, and an unbalanced Yin approach to life would be uninvolved, the Tao is the balancing point. Known simply in China as "the Way." The Way, or the Tao, is at the point of most power in golf and in all of life.

Overly Yin: tied to the past. Overly Yang: projected to the future. Balanced in the Tao: a blending of masculine and feminine attributes. In the now. At the point of most power which extends from the now infinitely in all directions. Point your finger into the sky. How far does that direction go? A Taoist golfer is always connected to the infinite, by being in the now.

Here is one example of how the Taoist principles act within nature. This is the Tao as seen within a solar system. The momentum of the planets can be seen as active ... Yang, masculine. The gravity of the sun attractive... Yin, feminine. The balance between the active nature (momentum) of the planets and the attractive nature (gravity) of the sun is where the Tao can be found. For it is the unseen Tao which maintains the balancing relationship, and therefore creation. All of creation is dependent upon balance. If the Yang aspect became too dominant, the momentum of the planets would move faster and faster, finally spinning off randomly into space. If the Yin aspect became too dominant, the gravity (attraction) would grow stronger and stronger until the planets were drawn into the center of the solar system and ultimately consumed by the sun. The same illustration can be made when analyzing the atomic structure, in this case substituting the planets with electrons and the sun with the nucleus of the atom.

Tao is born of Wu-Chi - 'the ultimate nothingness.' Tao is the mother of Yin and Yang. If they move, they separate; if they remain static, they combine.

-*Chinese Proverb*

In the martial arts, such as Kung Fu or Tai Chi Chuan, all movements and energy originate from the center of balance within the human body (which can be found directly below the navel.) This center is referred to in the Chinese martial arts as the Dantien. The Dantien can be considered to express the Tao of the body. If your body were a solar system, then the Dantien would be the sun. Emanating from the Dantien are channels of energy that flow throughout the bodily system in a way which is in some ways similar to the circulatory system and the nervous system of the body. This life energy which flows through the body is known as "Chi." It is precisely these channels of "Chi" which comprise the system of acupuncture meridians in the body. This system is at the basis of the ancient Chinese classic of medicine which found its origin in the Chow Dynasty in the year 696 B.C. In general, Chinese healing has to do with allowing Chi energy to flow properly and in a balanced fashion throughout the body. It is a system of healing which has maintained the well-documented health and longevity of the Chinese culture for thousands of years. In the Tao of golf, it will be a primary purpose to become aware of and access this powerful inner source of unlimited Chi energy. It is the Dantien which is at the hub of the wheel, which is your body.

> *Thirty spokes converge upon a single hub; it is*
> *on the hole in the center that the use of the*
> *cart hinges. We make a vessel from a lump of*
> *clay; it is the empty space within the vessel*
> *that makes it useful. We make doors and*
> *windows for a room; but it is these empty*
> *spaces that make the room livable. Thus, while*
> *the tangible has advantages, it is the intangible*
> *that makes it useful.*
>
> *- Tao Teh Ching*

The immense potential of Chi energy was demonstrated beautifully to me one day in New York City's Chinatown when I was visiting the herb shop and Tai Chi Dojo of Dr. Cheng Man Ching. (A Dojo is a center for the practice of the martial arts.) Dr. Cheng (now deceased) was famous in China and known as "the master of the five excellences," one of these five excellences being the martial art: Tai Chi Chuan. I was at his Dojo with my friend Herbert, who is an accomplished black belt in Karate. Herbert struck a strong contrast as he stood next to Dr. Cheng in the Dojo room. Dr. Cheng was slender, elderly, perhaps a foot shorter, and at least one hundred pounds lighter than Herbert. Herbert is tall with red hair and a loud, boisterous personality. Dr. Cheng, refined, quiet, and yet emanating a "presence" which seemed to overflow the space in which we were standing. Herbert, in his inquisitive way, began questioning the advantages of Tai Chi in comparison to other martial arts. In the way of providing an all-encompassing answer, Dr. Cheng instructed Herbert to move him from his spot. After a quizzical look, Herbert agreed to try.

In this attempt by Herbert, it appeared that no resistance was being exerted by the doctor. Yet as much as Herbert pushed, strained and groaned, no movement resulted. The doctor remained stationary and relaxed. Finally the doctor said to Herbert: "A wise man is a very intelligent man, but a sage knows where and when to stop." As Dr. Cheng uttered the word "stop" he placed a light tap with his fingers on the center of Herbert's chest. As I stood and watched in amazement, my 220 pound friend literally seemed to "soar" several feet across the room, landing harmlessly in an awkward heap on a pile of cushions. What a laugh we all shared after this astounding demonstration of the mastery of the Chi force.

Only when you can be extremely pliable and
soft, can you be extremely hard and strong.

-Zen Proverb

It is clear that this same inherent Chi that Dr. Cheng demonstrated for us is a major reason why all of the greatest masters of the game of golf appear to swing so effortlessly. The movement comes not from outer exertion, but from internal power and energy: the Tao of the body. Within this Tao is found limitless energy, grace, intricate beauty and unlimited potential. Golf, when truly practiced as a Taoist exercise, becomes a mysterious experience in the quest for perfection. So, let us now begin our adventure together into the Tao of golf.

Concentrate your mind inside your navel.
Penetrate the truth. Life and death are an out
and out lie.

- Zen Proverb

The Tai Chi Turn

Prior to offering any input regarding the actual physical process involved in playing the *Tao of Golf*, I must stress again that this book is not about the teaching of mechanics. However, it is of importance that you have the right mechanics integrated into your game from the very beginning as a Taoist golfer.

 Regardless of the strength of the horse, or the knowledge of the driver, no cart will move well ,with wheels that are square.

The Taoist golf swing must be an uncomplicated, straight forward, athletic move, patterned after the type of swing used by top professional golfers. It is important to utilize a standard grip, a proper stance, appropriate golfing posture and motion. If you do not feel that your swing conforms to the above standards, then it is my suggestion that you first acquire lessons from a carefully chosen PGA teaching professional. You will then be ready to address the immensely significant inner aspect of "Tao" of the game.

Although golf is largely a mental game, I also must emphasize that without the proper foundation of good fundamentals and technique, your success at the mental game will be limited to the degree of your physical preparedness. It is a basic Taoist precept to say, "As above, so below." In this case, the above is the mental game and the below is the physical game. The two will reflect one another. Having a good, relaxed, yet disciplined physical approach to the game indicates a relaxed and disciplined mental approach. Also, discipline and relaxation can be seen in the context of Yin and Yang. The discipline being experienced as active and Yang, while the relaxation can be seen as attractive and Yin. The Tao, or balance between these two qualities, provides for a free-flowing, yet focused performance. This is something which is extremely valuable on the golf course and elsewhere in life. All of your very finest performers in any field of endeavor will have a mastery of this combination of discipline and relaxation.

Even for the beginner, it should only take a few lessons (between three and five) to mentally learn the basic mechanics of an optimum golf swing. From there it is merely a question of practice, repetition and refinement. Said repetition will serve to train your body to execute the standard swing without active mental interference. As you repeat the correct swing, you are in essence assigning the mental information that you received from your instructor into data which is then embodied physically. It is within this transference of responsibility from mind to body that muscle memory replaces the need for memorization by the mind. The mind is incapable of independently swinging a golf club. It must rely upon the body to perform this, and all physical activities.

Therefore, it is essentially the body which must become trained, adept, and "intelligent."

When choosing a PGA professional as your instructor, it is important to find one who has a successful track record with his or her students. If at all possible, find a pro who is sought after by other professional golfers. Secondly, find a pro who is aware of, and in agreement with the need for inner awareness regarding the game of golf. If you find a teacher who is convinced that golf is all mechanics and no mental training is required, it will be more difficult for you to integrate his or her instruction with the Tao of golf.

Your eyes, nose and limbs may all work well,
but be careful: heaven and hell depends wholly
on your mind.

-Zen Proverb

Once you feel totally comfortable with the mechanics of your swing, you are then prepared to assimilate the esoteric approach to golf. The Tao of golf describes another deeper dimension of the game. It is the causal dimension.

Currently, it is the approach of many of the top-teaching professionals, and even touring pros such as Curtis Strange and Nick Faldo, to state that an important aspect of the golf swing is that the "inside must move the outside." That is, in other words, the large interior muscles of the torso, hips, thighs, back and shoulders should "swing" the smaller exterior muscles of the arms, wrists and hands, which in turn then swings the club. This idea is directly in keeping with the Taoist principle, except for the fact that with the Taoist swing or "Tai Chi Turn," it is the internal Chi energy which moves those larger muscles, which then moves the smaller exterior muscles... for this we must go one step within. Also, it is proper balance, breathing, concentration and awareness which will increase and activate the Chi.

There are several ways to increase and activate the Chi flow within your body. However, to most fully activate this energy, the recommendation is to begin the practice of Tai Chi Chuan under a qualified teaching master. As you develop your skills in Tai Chi, you will discover a great benefit to the game of golf. Tai Chi is also attributed to longevity, good health and greater zest for life in general. Since Tai Chi is based upon flowing movements rather than static postures, it is somewhat unrealistic to attempt to learn it from a book. Tai Chi should be learned from a qualified instructor. One of my fellow practitioners of Tai Chi (when I was studying under the Tai Chi master Abraham Liu in San Diego), cured himself of acute arthritis through this practice.

If you do not have the time or inclination to study Tai Chi, then it would be valuable to at least seek out a Tai Chi instructor who will show you how to properly do a basic Tai Chi exercise called "circling palms." By just correctly doing this single non-strenuous exercise for 30 minutes a day, you can greatly increase the Chi energy flow within your body, the power in your golf game, and also your overall health.

Miracles are not contrary to nature, but only
contrary to what we know about nature.

-Saint Augustine

When the Chi is activated across the technically correct golf swing, your distance and accuracy will be greatly increased. In an exercise with Steven Dove, one of my golfing partners who has a three handicap, I asked that he hit five shots on the driving range, alternating first using his regular swing and then five more using his regular swing while incorporating what I call the "Tai Chi Turn." Once Steven became comfortable with the Tai Chi turn, the increase in distance was between 30 and 50 yards per drive with no loss of accuracy. This was quite an increase for someone who already hits the ball an average of 230 yards off the tee. I later decided to perform the same experiment with one of my elderly golfing friends, Hal Davis. Hal is 77 years old, and has a 19 handicap. Although Hal is fairly accurate, especially around the greens, he is always looking for ways to recapture some of the distance he used to have from the tee. The Tai Chi turn increased Hal's driving distance in excess of 30 yards per shot. Since then, I have performed the same experiment with women, children, and golfers of various ages and abilities. The results are consistently excellent. The basics of the Tai Chi turn come from the practice of the Tai Chi exercise called "circling palms." By simply practicing the circling palms movement for thirty minutes prior to play, I am sure you will soon see the difference.

In Tai Chi, it can be said that your body is the connecting point between heaven and earth. To achieve the Taoist perspective, and experience yourself as such a connecting point, it is necessary to align the body-mind in the proper way. As a Taoist golfer, the active (Yang) center of attention of the physical body must be in the Dantien, at the center of the belly. Motion should originate from there. The attractive (Yin) center of attention should be within the heart and emotions. The emotions should be positive, happy and "pure of heart." When we are happy and pure of heart, we attract positive result into our circumstances, as like attracts like. The third principle, Tao, or balance, should be centered in the mind, which is free of thoughts or ideas. In golf, the Tao focused mind is completely immersed in visualizing the moment of the swing, and the path of the ball. It is totally open, aware, alert, and balanced. When these three alignments are achieved, in combination with the technically correct golf swing, you are prepared to engage the Tao of golf: active awareness in the Dantien, attractive sense of well-being in the heart, and balanced visualization in the mind. What follows is a more in depth understanding of the three aspects or the "three brains" as they are attributed to a Taoist understanding in the game of golf.

The Third Brain:

Physical Awareness; Chi Flow

When developing the physical portion of your swing through centering in the Dantien, a certain viewpoint is highly advantageous. It is the attitude of the warrior. In ancient Oriental times, a true warrior was expected to be noble, staunch, steadfast, disciplined, confident, moral, free of fear, and bold. These are the qualities which can be adopted when developing the Dantien. Yet, it is paradoxical, because in actuality, as the Dantien is developed, these qualities become the natural result. It is not really something to be thought about or planned. It is merely something to observe as the Dantien is developed.

If a golfer is developed in the physical (Yang) Dantien aspect of the game but not in balance with the emotional (Yin) or the mental (Tao) of the game, imbalances will result. An imbalanced Yang player will usually be very intense and prone toward anger, often a long hitter with a lack of emphasis on accuracy. He will have the tendency to be an aggressive chipper and putter who will go for the hole and will either make the putt or be way past. He will also have a tendency to "under club" (take less club than the distance requires) and then swing too hard. Furthermore, an imbalanced Yang player will have the tendency to swing too hard in general. In summary, an overly Yang player is a tense player.

The Second Brain:

Emotional Awareness; Positive Feelings

When we are happy, we attract success to ourselves. This is the premise in the Tao of golf. If we maintain a joyful spirit as we play the game of golf, this is where the true magic lies. It comes from really appreciating what we are doing. Happy, positive emotions are Yin (attractive). They attract positive results to us. They magnetize our being just as like attracts like. In golf, this is where the true magic comes from. The happy player is the one who will execute astounding shots, sink unbelievable putts, recover from difficult positions, and fully enjoy the challenge of the game, the company, the beauty of the course, and nature.

A golf course is an easy place to develop happy feelings. What the game of golf is, at one level, is a beautiful walk in a magnificent garden with your friends. You simply enjoy the company of your fellow golfers. But most of all, once you have developed a balanced game, golf itself becomes increasingly enjoyable.

As all golfers will tell you, golf is a challenging and difficult game to master. Most golfers never do achieve any degree of mastery. However, once you have developed a balanced Taoist approach to the game, you will find that your potential by far exceeds prior expectations. At that point, you can really begin to greatly enjoy the golf game itself. Herein lies still another paradox, because to really enjoy the game of golf it is very helpful to be a balanced player. Yet the best way to become balanced from the emotional standpoint, is to enjoy the game fully, regardless of your current level of progress. The golfer who has truly developed this aspect of their game walks with their head held high, observing and looking for beauty and absorbing the enjoyment of the moment. This is a key to developing the Yin aspect of your Taoist game.

As you experiment with maintaining a happy, joyful outlook, regardless of the results, you may be surprised to see how many effortless shots you begin to make. However, this will only work well for you if the Yin aspect of the game is maintained in harmony with the other two aspects: Yang and Tao, thus establishing the great Taoist synergy. Synergy, by definition, occurs when any totality is exponentially greater then the sum parts. When one is immersed in a state of Taoist synergistic awareness, they will by nature, express mastery. This type of mastery on the golf course will inevitably lead one far beyond any limited expectations.

A golfer who is imbalanced on the Yin side of the game can become too carefree, lax, careless and indifferent. This lack of focus is very detrimental to the game of golf (which truly requires heightened concentration). Whereas the overly Yang player is too tense, the overly Yin player is prone toward being too loose and passive. Therefore, in the Tao of golf, the prime focus is on balance. This balance is provided from beyond the mind. It comes from the overview, the silent observer.

The First Brain:
Mental Awareness-Visualization

The ideal state of mind for golf during the process of actually addressing the ball, is void of thought forms. This is true whether you are putting, chipping, driving or hitting a fairway shot. It is a mind concentrated on visualizing every shot without mental qualification, simply seeing and imagining exactly where you want that shot to go. It is seeing an imaginary line or arc which extends from the point of impact precisely to the target point. Not thinking about that line, or whether you feel that you can actually hit the ball along it, simply see the line without any conceptualization.

Eastern Oriental philosophy views the mind in a much different manner than we do in the West. In Taoism, the physical brain and nervous system are truly understood to a "terminal point" for a much greater universal mind. Somewhat like a single computer which is linked into a greater network. Another analogy is that the mind is a drop of water in the ocean of universal consciousness. The drop of water is made of the same basic substance, and has the same basic nature. The only true difference is the perspective of the "whole." The drop of water cannot truly experience its oceanic nature until it surrenders its attachment to it illusion of separateness. In much the same way, Eastern thought teaches us to surrender our self possession with the small issues of our egoic nature so that we can perceive the greatness of the whole of which we are not only an integral part, but also a microcosm.

*When a wise scholar hears the Tao, he
practices it diligently. When a mediocre
scholar hears the Tao, he wavers between
belief and unbelief. When a worthless scholar
hears the Tao, he laughs boisterously at it. But
if such a one does not laugh at it, the Tao
would not be the Tao!*

*The wise men of old have truly said: the bright
way looks dim. The progressive way looks
retrograde. The smooth way looks rugged.
High virtues look like an abyss. Great
whiteness looks spotted. Abundant virtue
looks deficient. Established virtue looks
shabby. Solid virtue looks as though melted.
Great squareness has no corners. Great talents
ripen late. Great sound is silent. Great form is
shapeless. The Tao is hidden and nameless;
yet it alone knows how to render help
and to fulfill.*

- Tao Teh Ching

In Taoism, the human mind is not considered to be limited to the brain or cranial area. It is understood among Taoists that the human mind is a system within the body which includes the brain as well as the entire nervous system of the physical body. Therefore, in Taoism it is not merely the cranial area which holds the capacity for thought, under-standing, or intellect. It is the entire body, with each part of the body perceiving or "thinking" in a manner which is unique to its particular role in the organism, that as an entire microcosm, thinks and perceives. This "thinking body" is essential to the Taoist approach to golf, because if our entire body becomes "intelligent" we are then able to exercise the precise and elegant muscle control necessary to excel in the game of golf.

To truly experience this holistic consciousness of which the body is comprised, it becomes necessary to first de-emphasize the conceptual mind in our approach to the Tao of golf. We must go beyond ideas and words and delve into the realm of direct experiential awareness. When swinging a golf club, not only should we feel each part of the body, we should also "listen" to each part of our entire being.

Exercise

Go to the driving range and take out your favorite club. After stretching and warming up, begin to methodically hit the golf balls as you concentrate on your various body parts. Do not worry about how far you are hitting the balls, or how straight. Simply concentrate on the inner "feel" of each shot. Begin with your feet and hands.

1. As you hit your first three shots, feel only your feet and hands, and limit your mind to one thought. Think: "goals."

Do not think about what your goals are. Simply think and repeat to yourself if this helps: "goals." The main focus is on the *feel*. Follow this same approach as you go through each of the following sections of your body.

2. With your next three shots, place your attention completely on your calves and forearms. *Feel* only your calves and forearm and think: "means."

3. With your next three shots, place your entire attention in your knees and elbows. *Feel* only your knees and elbows and think: "presentation."

4. With your next three shots, place your entire attention in your thighs and upper arms and think: "capacity."

5. With your next three shots, place your entire attention on your pelvic region and think: "potency and thrust."

6. With your next three shots, place the entirety of your attention in your abdomen and think: "balance and power."

7. With your next three shots, place the entirety of your attention in your chest and think: "impulse and desire."

8. With your next three shots, place the entirety of your attention in your lower back and think: "support and movement."

9. With your next three shots, place the entirety of your attention in your upper back and shoulders and think: "freedom."

10. With your next three shots, place the entirety of your awareness in your neck and jaw and think: "determination."

11. With your next three shots, place the entirety of your awareness in your mouth, throat and stomach and think: "needs."

12. With your next three shots, place the entirety of your awareness in your nose and lungs and think: "possibilities."

13. With your next three shots, place the entirety of your awareness in your eyes and think: "visualization."

14. With your next three shots, place the entirety of your awareness in your ears and think: "substance."

After you have consciously taken one hundred and eight shots with your *full attention* in each of these body parts, you will have begun the process of enlightening the body-mind for the purpose of becoming a Taoist golfer. This is a major step in developing the "feel" necessary to becoming a true Taoist golfer.

For the purpose of clarification, I am not suggesting that you alternate the focus of your awareness across these different body parts while you are on the course. This is strictly an exercise for the practice range. Remember, while playing a round of golf the Taoist golfer is active (Yang), physically with attention centered in the lower abdomen. Attractive (Yin) emotionally with a pure and open heart. Balanced (Tao) in the mind as the silent observer visualizing each shot.

For the Taoist golfer, practice and play are two entirely different processes. In practice we are disciplining the mind and the body. In actual play, we are relaxed and allowing, yet totally focused within the moment.

The Quest for Balance

A time honored Taoist precept is the understanding that "the outside world is a pure reflection of the inner world." All outer circumstances are specifically attracted into our life by our level of consciousness. If good things are happening around us, that reflects a positive interior state. If difficulties are common to our external environment, that suggests confusion, contradiction, or difficulties regarding our interior level of awareness. The Taoist understands this. Awake consciousness is reflected by a harmonious life. Asleep consciousness is reflected with contradictions in life. It is for this reason that the true Taoist takes full responsibility for his or her life. This is the nature of a mature Taoist practitioner.

With this precept in mind, golf functions as an excellent mirror. Each golf shot gives us specific and immediate feedback about our consciousness at the moment of the shot. If we are balanced and centered, our golf shot will reflect that, and fly true and straight toward its target. If we are imbalanced Yang, perhaps the shot will be hit "too fat" below the ball, or be pulled or hooked off line. When we are balanced, centered, clear, and aware, with each of the three "brains" working together in harmony, our golf shots can reflect that clarity and level of consciousness.

In both the game of golf, and the game of life, an important initial step is to identify your game. The key to improvement is self awareness. Do not try to deny the weak parts of your game and think only of the strengths. Embrace your wholeness and become objective to all aspects. In seeking the balance, begin with a balanced mental perspective. See your game from the Taoist perspective, with objective dispassionate analysis. Do not judge those parts of your game which require improvement, nor applaud those aspects which are more developed.

It is valuable to actually dedicate three to five rounds of golf on the following exercise: Simply observing yourself without concern for results. Simply get to know your game. Is it imbalanced Yin? Is it imbalanced Yang? In what ways are you moving toward center? Toward balance? Toward aligning your game with the flow of nature and the universe?

*To be out of the flow is like standing at the
edge of a river, pointing upstream and yelling at
the top of your lungs: 'Go that way.' Neither
the river, nor the Tao will respond. But when
the Tao or the river is embraced, and flowed
with rather than against, great power can be
discovered.*

By maintaining a pure clarity of awareness as you golf you may well be amazed at the control you have over your game, and your shots. If you allow this same conscious approach to overflow into everyday life, you will notice once again how the inside reflects the outside. As you live more and more as a Taoist with your three centers in balance, your entire life's experience will improve much in the same way that your golf game does. This improvement will be seen in your health, vitality, joy of life, relationships, prosperity, creativity, intellect, and ability to hit it down the middle of life's fairway in all worthy endeavors.

Yang

*Creative, masculine, centered physically in the
Dantien. Chi flow. Power. Energy.
Potency of Action.*

Imbalanced Yang

Projected into the future.

Yin

Creation. Attractive. Feminine. Mysterious.
Centered emotionally in the heart. Beauty.
Purity. Joy. Peace. Nature.

Imbalanced Yin

Tied to the past.

Tao

Universal awareness. The all encompassing
now as the point of most power. Conscious-
ness, and joy which infinitely extend in all
directions into forever. The balance of body,
mind, and emotion. Visualization. Manifes-
tation. Creator. Creativity. Creation.

With all of this in mind, I am sure the question arises, "How does one obtain and develop balance within the three centers?" I must first say that is definitely a matter of degree. Taoism is a process and not a goal. To be a Taoist is not to reach anywhere, nor to aspire toward any specific result. The true Taoist, flows without contradiction, flowing with nature, flowing with the universe. It is impossible to point at any human being, no matter how adept that individual might be, and say that he or she has obtained a perfect, final development and balance of the physical, emotional and mental centers. To the Taoist, there is always somewhere to go. Nothing is finite. There is no final goal.

 It is never too late to be what you might have
been.

- George Elliot

So, it is possible to develop these three centers, and to bring them into greater and greater balance, but there is no limit with regard to this development. By beginning this process of balancing and therefore enlightening the three centers, it can be said that you are beginning a pathway into the infinite. There will always be room for improvement, and the improvement that you experience can be quite remarkable.

The Dantien

The Point of Most Power

- Gathering the Now -

An example of one way in which the Dantien can function

Several years ago, I was sitting at a lecture by the Dean of the University for Humanistic Studies in San Diego. There were perhaps eight or nine hundred people in attendance, and I was sitting toward the rear. The Dean was talking about the work of Peter Caddy, one of the founders of the Findhorn Community in Northern Scotland. I, on the other hand (although interested in the wonderful Findhorn Community) had an additional motive for being at the lecture. It was my desire to talk to some of the people there and promote a seminar I was preparing to conduct at the university. It was one day before the ten-week seminar was scheduled to start, and I had only 28 students. For it to go forward, I required at least 33 participants, so basically, although I was interested in Findhorn, I was also at the lecture to do PR.

From my seat in the rear, I decided to perform an experiment using the Dantien. I began to breathe very deeply, quietly and slowing. Inhaling through the nose, I imagined the sound of the ocean surf as it draws back from the shore. And then, exhaling through my mouth, I imagined the sound of the waves crashing in against the shore. As I continued this breathing, I visualized the entire room filled with a sea of energy. As I inhaled, all of that energy was drawn into the Dantien of my body. As I exhaled, I imagined that the energy was greatly increased, and then returned to the room filling it with love, light and positive healing energies. While I continued this exercise (which I now call Ocean Breathing), I focused all of my attention upon that moment. I allowed no thoughts to enter my head other than the oceanic imagery.

The result of my experiment was amazing, yet at first subtle. I noticed that although I was toward the back of the large meeting room, it seemed as if the speaker was addressing more and more of her comments directly to me. It was as if we were having a private conversation. As this continued, the speaker began to look only at me as she talked. Next, the subject matter of her lecture changed, and she was no longer speaking about Peter Caddy or Findhorn. Instead, she was discussing her excitement about my upcoming seminar. Remarkably, she then announced my presence in the audience, and asked me to come up to the podium to speak about the seminar.

I was quite amazed at this opportunity, as I had only expected to pass out flyers as people exited the lecture. Instead, I was invited up front to tell everyone about the program. Out of courtesy and appreciation, I discussed the seminar's similarities (there were several) to the work that was being done at Findhorn. Following my short address and the program, I had over two hundred applicants from the audience. My next three seminars were filled in advance to capacity. I attribute none of this result to myself, or any unique qualities that I might have, but rather to the power and potential of the Dantien. It is a potential which everyone has. A potential which is used widely in the martial arts, and can be of utmost value in the game of golf. The golfer who is playing while using the power of the Dantien will express greater power and accuracy. It will seem effortless.

A direct way to activate the Dantien is with deep breathing and concentration in the lower abdomen, about two finger widths below the navel. Other ways include physical exercises from the martial arts and the usage of intonations. However, as you can imagine, doing the slow, dance-like movements of Tai Chi while sitting in an audience, or making low deep tones while concentrating in the lower belly might have been construed as inappropriate when listening to the lecture.

Emotions

The key to being a Taoist golfer from the emotional stand-point involves enjoying the process without attachment to particular results. It involves having a sense of humor about ourselves while also focusing on the mystery of connectedness with all that is. When we feel the heart connection with all things, we are immediately able to function in harmony. When functioning in true harmony with nature and the universe, we are opening ourselves to the mysterious, unexpected and the exciting. It involves seeing and feeling everything as alive, and realizing that everything around you is sensitive to the impact of your presence.

> *There is a light that shines beyond all things on*
> *earth, beyond us all, beyond the heavens,*
> *beyond the highest, the very highest heavens.*
> *This is the light that shines in our heart.*
> *- Chandogya Upanishad*

I quite tangibly experienced this feeling of connectedness upon return to the country club in Santa Maria, California, where I played golf as a boy. I had not been back to that lovely course in over twenty years. I was feeling an emotional peak about returning there, and being able to play the course again. It was like returning to visit a dear old friend.

I arrived on an early autumn evening, and the pro shop was about to close. When I went in, my old high school friend Jim was working there as an assistant pro. He greeted me as if he had just seen me yesterday, rather than two decades ago. Since the Santa Maria Country Club is a private course, I required permission to play. Jim said, "sure." I tried to pay him, but he would not accept. It seemed that he sensed how happy I was to be there, and how special this was for me. It was a gift.

I believe that there may be nothing more effective in golf, than to play with joy. This will bring you naturally to the peak of your potential.

When I stepped up on the first tee at Santa Maria Country Club, the course was silent and still. I looked down the number one fairway. I had played this shot so often as a youth, and I was that youth again. I took a practice swing but it did not feel as if I was swinging the golf club. It felt as if I was being swung. The feeling was ecstatic, like the club knew what to do. No thought or decision was needed. I looked at the spot on the fairway which is an ideal landing area. My club swung, and the ball soared as straight as an arrow, directly to that spot. Everything seemed to be in slow motion. The sound of the club striking the ball was immense, like a thunder clap. The golf course gasped in pleasure as the ball soared through the air. I felt as if I was one with the course, as if this was a love affair. I felt welcomed into the arms of the course. As I hit each shot, it flew to the exact area that I was visualizing. As you can imagine, although I only had limited daylight, it was the best score for five holes that I have ever scored on that course, or any other. I was five under par. Joy has an immense impact upon our success in golf and in life in general. The Taoist golfer plays golf joyfully and then witnesses the magic.

Attain to the utmost emptiness.
Cling single-heartedly to interior peace. While
all things are stirring together,
only contemplate the return. For flourishing as
they do, each of them will return to its root. To
return to the root is to find peace. To find
peace is to fulfill one's destiny. To fulfill one's
destiny is to be constant. Top know the
constant is called insight. If one does not
know the constant, one runs blindly into
disasters. If one knows the constant, one can
understand and embrace all.
If one understands and embraces all, one is
capable of doing justice. To be just is to be
kingly; to be kingly is to be heavenly; to be
heavenly is to be one with the Tao. To be one
with the Tao is to abide forever. Such a one
will be safe and whole even
after the dissolution of the body.

- Tao Teh Ching

The Mind

Your golf game will improve dramatically when you are fully able to visualize each shot. To "see" exactly how you wish for the ball to fly toward its target, then to fly it there without doubt or hesitation. This is at the center of the capability of the mind. To perceive, and then conceive. The mind must be clear. It must be focused in the present moment of the shot. There can be no negative thought forms or doubts, as all doubts and negative "self talk" will manifest themselves into your game. The golfer needs to leave the prior shot behind, regardless of whether it was excellent, awful or somewhere in between. Each golf shot requires the total attention of the mind within that moment. This is the mental Tao of golf. It is the removal from your thoughts of desires, goals and ulterior motives. It is also the removal of self blame, or negative self talk. It is simply the joy of being "inside the feel." The joy of "flying." When your mind visualizes a shot and then your body responds by executing that shot, the mind is able to fly along the trajectory of the shot. In this way it can be said that golf in a sense, fulfills man's ancient, historic and genetic desire to physically be able to fly.

The Mental Game

By releasing the mind from the specific it is allowed to encompass the all. The paradox of 'bringing the mind to a single point of attention' is that the focused relaxation of the mind can travel through that single point to encompass the entire universal viewpoint. The mind is then at its height of power. Unencumbered and free, open to all because it is empty, receptive, attractive and magnetic.

The Taoist golfer's mental game involves the releasing of the specific, to encompass and embrace the all. Rather than focusing on any particular thought while playing, the Taoist is involved in seeing and experiencing the whole. Within each shot, the Taoist is always a beginner, authentic, intelligent and objective.

Our Mind, and every kind of jewel. If you
polish them, they will shine accordingly.

- Zen Proverb

Finally, regarding the mind and golf, it must be said that it is the mind which determines your level of confidence. If your mind has doubts about your ability to perform, your game will simply reflect those doubts. If your mind expects only the very best, your game will reflect that. We tend to hit the ball as well as we expect to hit it. My favorite example of this happened one day while I was playing with one of my golfing friends at my home course in Washington State.

Bill has a 22 handicap. He is seventy years old, and he plays golf almost every day. He therefore has developed some fairly specific expectations about his abilities and limitations. We were on the ninth hole, which is a Par 4 with a distance of 295 yards. Bill had what he thought was a fairly decent drive down the middle of the fairway. After his tee shot, he was about 130 yards from the green. Judging the distance, he said to me: "Oh good, I get to hit my favorite club. I always hit this club well." I asked him which club he was hitting and he said, "a six iron." Bill pulled out the club, and took a smooth, confident swing. The ball flew high in the air and then landed softly about four feet from the pin. I was surprised how high the shot went. Suddenly, Bill started laughing. "I don't believe it, " he said. "I thought I had the six iron, but I read it upside down. I just hit a nine iron!"

Bill, an elderly gentleman with a 22 handicap, had just hit a nine iron shot approximately the same distance, and with the same accuracy as a pro. Why was this? Because he *expected* to hit the ball well, and he expected it to go clear to the green. He thought he was hitting his favorite club, and he expected it to fly about 135 yards. Bill felt so confident that he could reach the green with the club in his hand, that he did. The power of the mind, vividly at work!

The Tao of Dubbing

 Welcome disgrace as a pleasant surprise. Prize
calamities as your own body.
Why should we 'welcome disgrace as a
pleasant surprise?' Because a lowly state is a
boon: getting it is a pleasant surprise, and so is
losing it! (cont'd)

That is why we should 'welcome disgrace as a pleasant surprise.' Why should we 'prize calamities as our own body?' Because our body is the very source of our calamities. If we have no body, what calamities can we have?

- Tao Teh Ching

All golfers must make peace with the fact that they will not always hit the ball exactly where or how they want to hit it. Ben Hogan once said, "you know that you are improving as a golfer when your misses are serviceable." This statement itself can be perceived in both an inner Yin and outer Yang manner. From the Yang standpoint, what Hogan probably meant was that a missed shot by an improved golfer will probably be more easily recovered from than a missed shot by a beginner. Or, he may have meant that what a professional golfer might consider a miss, a beginner might consider to be a great shot.

However, regardless of what Hogan meant, let's look at his statement from the Taoist point of view. From this perspective, we can say we know we are improving when we gain value from our misses, thereby making our missed shots more serviceable from the mental standpoint. The more we are able to learn, and therefore benefit from our mistakes in golf, and in life, the more we will improve the quality of our performance and experience.

As a Taoist golfer, when you are not hitting the ball the way you may wish to, you are confronted with an exceptional opportunity. It is the immediate opportunity to improve your game. Your missed hits are telling you something which is not only mechanical, but perhaps more significantly, mental. Perceive your game with the three aspects of the Tao as your general overview. Are your shots too Yin? Too Yang? Or balanced? This is a good overview. However, to truly gain knowledge, we must also be specific.

Listen to what you are mentally saying to yourself, especially after you hit a poor shot. Listen again before you hit the shot directly following the poor shot. Are you judging or blaming yourself? Are you angry with yourself? Judgment, blame and anger are all negative emotions which will serve to remove you from a state of internal equilibrium, thereby taking you out of the Tao. The Taoist golfer objectively observes all golf shots without attachment or value judgment. If it is a good shot it is pleasurable, but with less to be learned. If it is a poor shot, then there is opportunity. The Taoist becomes acutely alert and aware of the three centers of the body, and where the imbalance is originating. From the physical standpoint, the Taoist will look at mechanics, energy flow of the body and how connected they feel to the earth and nature. From the emotional standpoint, the Taoist will observe feelings. How he or she is feeling emotionally about the game, about the day, the company, and life in general at that moment. From the mental standpoint, how acute is the concentration of awareness and visualization centered in the current moment in time?

> *If I do it like this, the result will be like this.*
> *But fully knowing that, I'm suffering like*
> *this ...*
>
> *- Zen Proverb*

Some golfers are only slightly "out of the moment" with their concentration. Perhaps they are thinking of the good or bad shot that they hit on the prior hole. For example, "I hit that last shot well; maybe I can repeat what I did then and hit this one the same way." This type of thinking is slightly out of the moment, and therefore out of the Tao. Each shot deserves specific and individual attention without regard to past or present.

Another slightly out of the moment thought might be about an especially challenging golf hole coming up. Something like, "I better do well on this hole, because the next hole is really tough, and I might not score well on it." In this example, the golfer is not only out of the moment and out of the Tao, he or she is also programming the subconscious mind for failure on the future hole. Chances are, both holes will be less successful than desired.

Right now, right here, today. That's your
business. Yesterday has gone forever.
Tomorrow has not yet come.

- Zen Proverb

Sometimes a golfer will be extremely out of the moment. For example, thinking about a business deal that happened the prior week, a relationship, or somewhere that he or she has to go later. In this case, the golfer is wholly out of connection with the Tao. This is the time when the Taoist golfer should ask, "What is going on in my life that is distracting me from my game?" Very often, this will lead to insights about dubbed shots, especially if the performance is below normal. Clear the mind of concerns which are not relevant to the particular shot and moment at hand.

Each golf shot must be experienced as an "individual universe" unto itself. Total attention, balance, awareness and respect must be afforded to all shots, even ones which appear to be easy. Even if it is a short chip from an easy lie, or simply a ten inch putt. Very often, it is the easier shots which can be dubbed. This is often caused by a lack of attention to detail, which is a lack of presence. The golfer may have thought the shot was automatic, having made it several times before. They therefore might well swing without focused awareness. These occasions are great learning opportunities. What do you mentally say to yourself after missing such a shot? Do you call yourself a name? Do you curse yourself? Not if you are the Taoist golfer, because as a Taoist, you have just learned a great lesson in concentration, and it only cost you a single stroke. What a bargain!

Today's praise, tomorrow's abuse: it's the
human way. Weeping ..laughing ...
all utter lies.

- Zen Proverb

The Taoist golfer always accepts that there is room for improvement. There is a sense of humility involved. The Taoist golfer does not believe that he or she will automatically always excel at golf or at life. The Taoist approaches both life and golf with respect, honor and humility. The Taoist golfer also has a great sense of humor regarding self. You will find that they enjoy themselves regardless of the particular results of the day. By their emotional appearance, you will not be able to determine whether they have shot a 68 or a 98. This is the Tao of dubbing.

Stress

What are stress, suffering and difficulties in
life (or on the golf course) all about?
At one level they are about not being who we
truly are at the moment of the trauma.
At another level it is a message from life about
a need for an adjustment in perspective,
attitude, assumption, or behavior with regard
to who we truly are.

"Benephobia"

Many people perform far below their true potential. They simply do not allow themselves to excel or improve to any particular degree, nor do they allow themselves to express their innate abilities. They suffer from what I like to call "Benephobia." The fear of beneficial circumstances.

On the golf course, an individual who is chronically suffering from benephobia will tend to follow a birdie with a double bogey. If they play the front side well, they will do poorly on the back side. They have a subconscious dedication to mediocrity. They believe that something good is inevitably followed by something bad. This is often based on some kind of early childhood programming which has mistakenly informed the individual that they are not worthy of abundance, prosperity, or beneficial circumstances. As long as an individual suffers from "Benephobia" they will be unable to really fulfill their dreams in life, whatever those might be. The mental fear of beneficial circumstances will result in the subconscious creation of less than desirable results. They will be unable to truly progress, no matter what the field of endeavor.

Indeed, "Benephobia" is a negative type of mental conditioning that many have learned early in life. But to embody such an unconscious belief in mediocrity also requires your agreement. If you feel that you have accepted less from yourself or life than your potential would dictate, it is time to kick the "benephobia" habit. To do so takes conscious attention, especially at times when things are going their very best. Be aware of any thought forms or mental attitudes which surface at successful moments which might be suggesting that "things are too good to be true", or "whatever goes up must come down," or "waiting for the other foot to drop," or whatever the negative attitude or assumption might be. Watch for these implications of Benephobia, and consciously disassociate yourself from any and all such thought forms which may arise. Persistently continue to succeed in times of success. Always assume that if things are going good, they will only get better, and better and better.

There is nothing in the universe which demands that positive experiences must be followed by negative experiences. It all depends upon the power of your consciousness, and more clearly, what you want, and what your expectations are. Continue to focus your attention on the positive result that you expect. It is a universal principle: that which you give your attention to increases, you get more of it. Always be fascinated by that which you desire to occur. You will indeed receive more of it. Then, in this way, the condition of Benephobia will naturally dissolve from your consciousness.

Too much of a good thing can be wonderful.

- Mae West

Highs and Lows

The Taoist golfer seeks the center point. In evaluating your own game, think about your "highs" and your "lows." One moment you will feel as if you are in a groove, and golf is the easiest game in the world. Every drive, every shot, every putt will go exactly where you want it to go. And you may wonder why you don't always play this well? It is so easy. Then, the other extreme comes into play. You cannot hit anything. You game is at its worst. You are totally frustrated. Yet you are the same golfer who in a different instance felt unlimited ease and ability. Why is this? From the Taoist viewpoint, you are expressing the extremes of your abilities and limitations.

Between ability and limitation exists balance. The Tao. It is not the function of the Taoist golfer to avoid, deny or suppress limitations. They must be integrated. The Taoist knows that his or her true ability will never be realized until these limitations are addressed. All golfers have limitations, from the top pro to the rankest amateur. The golfer who is aware of these limitations (even at times of top performance), and also aware of ability and potential (even at times of greatest limitation), will begin to approach the center point, the golfer's ideal, which is consistency.

As you reach this center point it begins to evolve into a greater and greater refinement. To the true Taoist golfer, the highs and lows become indistinguishable. They are contained within one another. Then the greatest and most stable progress is possible. The Taoist golfer will be a very consistent golfer. In the early stages of practice, the game may be modest. But the ability and potential of any golfer naturally increases with correct practice and repetition. The difference, in the case of the Taoist golfer, is that the awareness of limitations is integrated into the game at all times, along with the enjoyment of the advancing ability. This is a mature practitioner. This will result in a consistent performer whose development will be stable, steady, and grounded. It is the kind of improvement that will not regress back to a lesser degree of proficiency, due to suppression or ignorance of limitation.

The paradox is that the more one denies and/or ignores existing limitations, the more they become prevalent. On the other hand, the more one addresses and is aware of any limitations as they occur, the more they recede. It is the function of the conscious awareness to disperse such things as limitation, darkness, or negativity. To ignore such things cultivates them. It is not the suggestion here, to dwell upon limits, however. There is a clear distinction. Taoism is a process of bringing negative, or limiting energies to the light. This is done through objective, dispassionate awareness, and not through closing one's eyes and pretending that the limitation doesn't exist within the moment. Another thing to remember, from the Taoist viewpoint, is limitations are temporary, while awareness is eternal. When the temporal and the eternal are combined, only the eternal will remain.

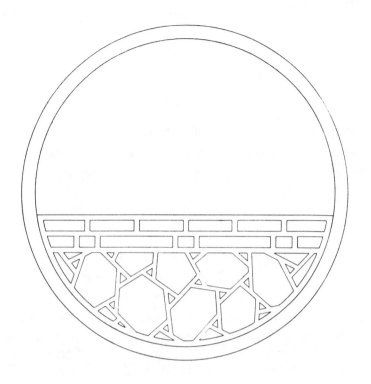

The Tao of Putting

It seems that in many cases, especially among amateurs, the very least attention, practice, and interest is placed upon mastering the art of putting. There are fewer books available, few tapes, and less time (if any) dedicated to teaching putting. This is a definite paradox in that more strokes are taken with the putter than any golf club in the bag, and putting constitutes 40% of all the strokes necessary for an even par round of golf (if all greens are reached in regulation). Although in almost all cases all greens are not reached in regulation, statistics show that on the pro tour, putting constitutes over 33% of golf shots taken. Most touring pros dedicate hours and hours weekly to practice on the putting green.

Putting: humble, lowly, close to the earth.

No great show. No great power ...

Supremely important.

The role of putting in golf truly exemplifies what Taoism is, and what a Taoist understands: "That which lies below, also stands above." A true Taoist golfer will be a great putter.

Greatness is like a lowland toward which all

streams flow. It is the reservoir of all under

heaven, the feminine of the world.

- Chinese Proverb

Putting is that part of the golf game which is an equalizer. Everyone can putt well regardless of their power, youth or gender. The frailest little child can putt with more skill and accuracy than the huge hitter, whose drives soar over 300 yards down the fairway. Putting brings the mental, awareness side of golf more clearly into play than any other aspect of the game.

Why is putting given less attention than other aspects of the game? Perhaps it is because putting represents the following significant Taoist paradox: "The highest is the simplest, and yet the simplest is the most difficult." This statement is called the master key of Tai Chi. It is so simple that it contains all other principles within it. When a non-Taoist hears this master key, he will perhaps laugh. When a non-adept Taoist hears this master key he may acknowledge it, yet forget to practice it. Only a few will achieve mastery of it, and their pathway will be impeccable. The master key is no short cut. Practice of the master key is the work of a lifetime.

The highest is the simplest, and yet, the

simplest is the most difficult.

- The Master Key of Tai Chi

Putting appears to be the simplest aspect of golf, but more clearly, it is the simplest to learn, but perhaps the hardest to master. A small child who has never golfed can immediately take a putter and roll the ball somewhat accurately toward the hole. Yet putting is of supreme importance to the game of golf, and this is still another reason why golfing is such a Taoist game. The one who is focused and connected to the earth will putt well. The one who is putting well will quite likely achieve success.

> *"Courage is grace under pressure."*
>
> *- Ernest Hemingway*

Tension can tend to mount for most golfers as they approach the putting green. They are aware of the fact that putting, more than any other aspect of golf, requires ultimate precision. Even the smallest error in touch or alignment can result in a missed putt. Furthermore, any extra three or four inch putt that becomes necessary to finally get the ball into the hole will cost the same on the score card as a 250 or 300 yard tee shot.

The Tao of "Taking Dead Aim"

Project your divine being into the hole,
visualize the hole as the magnetic center of the
universe. Allow the ball to be the evolving
aspect of your being. See it merge as it enters
the hole with that aspect of yourself which is
already fulfilled, complete, and waiting for you
at the center. Realize that the alchemical
marriage or reunion between the spirit self and
the material self is the natural result of all
human existence. The simplest sinking of a
putt to the Taoist golfer, when properly
focused in the moment,
exemplifies such an analogy.

Using Taoist knowledge, the tension which occurs within many golfers can be transferred into a higher focus of awareness. This can quite readily be done by utilizing a simple breathing exercise while focusing awareness in the Dantien. To eliminate tension in any aspect of life, the abdomen region needs to be totally relaxed, open and unconstrained. In Eastern civilization, breath control is an ancient and time-honored method for achieving relaxation and focus, while raising one's level of consciousness.

Exercise

This following exercise can be done inconspicuously as you walk down the fairway toward the green: Take nine very deep and very slow breaths as you focus the entirety of your awareness in the abdomen region. As you inhale, imagine that your are inhaling focused awareness. As you exhale, imagine that your are exhaling tension. Inhale awareness, exhale tension ... Inhale awareness, exhale tension ... nine times.

Once you have released the tension through the breath you are ready to get down to the business at hand. Taoist putting involves proper mechanics. The mechanical aspect can be perceived to be Yang, physical. Taoist putting requires trust in yourself, Yin, emotional. Taoist putting requires attention to detail, Tao, mental. If you have developed these three factors, you can be a great putter.

Mind, Tao

Attention to Detail

The attention to detail is paramount in putting. It involves the heightened awareness that comes from really "seeing" everything that is significant to your shot. Seeing the condition of the green: is it wet or dry? Is it soft or firm? Has it been recently mowed? What is the grain of the green? What kind of grass is it? Is it Bermuda? Is it bent grass? What is the slope of the green? If you were to take a five gallon bucket of water and pour it out onto the green, which way would the water flow? The direction of your putt will flow like water across the green.

Also, it is very valuable to be acutely aware of the roll of the ball of your playing partners. How hard did they strike the ball? How smoothly did it roll? Is the green fast or slow? Many golfers pay attention to the shots of others, if they feel that it will give them specific information about their particular line. This is fine. However, every shot that is taken on the green from any location will give the aware Taoist golfer input as to the nature of the surface and how to address the shot.

It is not necessary to actively draw conclusions regarding the information that you gather as you pay careful attention to details. Simply see everything. Allow all of the information to be absorbed without qualification, interpretation, or active mental activity. Remember, the function of the mind in the Tao of golf is visualization. Seeing and understanding without the need for active conceptualization. Active conceptualization causes the mind to become active rather than remaining balanced in the center between action and attraction. The Taoist mind is the balanced mind. The overview, the objective observer. The body, centered in the Dantien, must remain active rather than the mind. The mind is incapable of hitting the golf shot. It is the body that must do that. It is important for you to have trust in yourself and trust in your body's ability to intelligently perform. It is the function of the mind to see where the body needs to hit the ball. To see the line, to see the conditions of the green, to absorb all of the data that is available. It is then the function of the body to execute the shot. The mind must let go, and trust the body.

Heart, Yin

Trust in Yourself

Many golfers seem to believe that having a good "touch" around the green is a quality that some players are blessed with while others are not. From the Taoist perspective, however, it is the premise that all golfers who are conscious and aware are capable of having an excellent touch. Having a good "touch" is having good awareness of distance and space.

Distance awareness, from the Taoist perspective is inherant within the truly conscious being. This is simply because a conscious being, fully present in the moment, has objective awareness of time, and therefore space, which vibrates at the same frequency as time. "Good Touch" is the purest example of the function of consciousness in the putting process. It is strictly a function of awareness.

By being totally present in the moment while putting, chipping, or hitting any shot which requires a "feel" for distance, your body will simply *know* exactly how much energy and force is required. The less that the conceptual mind is involved with this process, the more precisely accurate you will become with regard to distance. The more that you trust your body's intelligence and awareness to *know this*, the more successful your sense of touch will become, to the very point of amazement and awe.

Body, Yang

Proper Mechanics

As stated before, it is not the purpose of this book to instruct you in the mechanics of golf or of putting. However, proper mechanics are of utmost importance. When it comes to putting mechanics, the greatest book that I know of is *Putt Like the Pros*, by David Pelz. To obtain a complete and excellent overview of proper putting mechanics, I highly recommend that book.

In essence, however, learning the basic fundaments will allow your putting stroke to be fully efficient and therefore not interfere with the capability for genius which is inherently contained within the consciousness of any aware individual. Having good basic mechanics is a sound foundation for success. Most pros agree that the putting stroke should be straight back and straight through, directly along the line of the putt. The arms should swing like a pendulum, using the arms and not the wrists. They recommend keeping the head still, yet relaxed. The putter should be aligned perfectly perpendicular to the line. The ball should be hit directly on the "sweet spot" of the putter. These are merely logical technical approaches which will make it easier for your body to perform naturally without attempting to compensate for any complications in your stroke. Taoism: *Strive for Simplicity.*

Putting Exercise

In order to provide your body with the proper "muscle memory" to repeat the technically correct stroke on the golf course without mental interference, the following repetition is recommended:

A. Place two phone books on the carpet leaving a parallel path between them that is just wide enough for your putter to stroke the ball through. Have the pathway between the two books be 1/8 of an inch wider than the width of your putter. This pathway will cause you to keep your putter on line straight back and straight through.

B. Hit 108 putts per day. Count only those putts in which your putter does not brush against either of the phone books. Make sure that you are hitting your putts on the "sweet spot" of the putter, without using your wrists. Do not be concerned about a target. You are merely providing your body with the proper mechanical muscle memory for a technically uncomplicated and correct putting stroke.

C. As you putt, remain still, yet relaxed, without concern about the distance of the putt or whether or not you are "accelerating through the putt." Make no unnecessary movements of the head and body.

Putting is not an exact science. No matter how well you perform the above-mentioned suggestions as a Taoist putter, there is still the chance that your putts will not go in. The putting green is an unpredictable place. It is affected by the amount of players who have walked across it on a given day, spike marks, irregularities in the grass, unseen wet or soft spots, and even the wind can effect a putt. The Taoist golfer approaches putting with humility, and yet with the security of knowing and expecting that they will be extremely successful if they are employing the proper principles of awareness.

The Practice Green

Many professional golfers spend up to an hour or more per day on the practice green, especially prior to a tournament. There is an old saying: "Practice makes Perfect." The Taoist golfer is one who carries this idea one step further, and in the words of Dave Stockton: "Perfect Practice makes

Perfect." It is extremely valuable to spend at least a half hour on the practice green prior to a match, tournament, or even a friendly round of golf.

Since a Taoist golfer is not goal oriented, the same importance and attention is assigned to each and every round of golf, regardless of any stake or rewards. Therefore, the practice and preparation routine remains the same. The Taoist golfer approaches the practice green to fine tune the three principle factors: mechanics, attention to detail, and trust in self. Most of the putts are hit from a distance of from ten to twenty-five feet to establish touch and and awareness of the type of surface at that particular course.

Mastery of putting is a huge step toward significantly improving your game. Although it is often underrated, precise putting can almost immediately take several strokes off your average scores. Why not become a great putter? You can do it! And remember, there is always room for improvement. Once you begin to gain confidence in your putting, it is important to maintain a routine of "perfect practice." You will get better and better.

The Tao of Golfing
with Others

Golf is a peaceful, non-combative sport. Therefore, it is on the golf course that you will find some of the finest, most thoughtful and aware people in our culture. Paramount to golf is proper etiquette and consideration for fellow golfers. This honorable and genteel approach is still another reason why golf can so ideally be considered a Taoist game.

Since golf does require a relatively high degree of concentration, unwritten rules have naturally evolved so that all players can perform without unnecessary distraction. There are certain things that the appropriate golfer simply wouldn't do, such as speak or make audible noises just as a fellow golfer is swinging or putting; step in another golfer's putting line; stand behind another golfer and in their direct line of sight when they are addressing the ball; stand directly behind the target when a fellow golfer is either chipping or putting; or stand with their shadow cast across a fellow golfer's putting line. These, of course, are not all of the rules of etiquette. However, they are some of the most commonly known and practiced.

The Tai Chi of Gamesmanship

The golf course is a great place for people to enjoy the matching of wills, competitiveness and ability. Because we live in such a competitive society, it is only natural that this aspect would be reflected on the golf course. People love to compete, they love to win, they hate to lose. It is a primary dichotomy of our culture.

Although the Taoist golfer is involved in an inner process which really isn't overly concerned with winning or losing, they will often find themselves in situations where they are playing with others who enjoy this competitive aspect. A Taoist golfer feels that the game is already won if they are playing from the universal perspective. A Taoist golfer could easily win a golf match and yet feel a sense of loss if they did not play consciously. On the other hand, a Taoist could lose a match and yet feel great about the game if the game was played at a high level of awareness.

When golfing with others in a competitive situation, the Taoist might often be confronted with the phenomena which is known as "Gamesmanship." Loosely described, "gamesmanship" refers to a process in which an opponent might attempt to undermine your confidence, or in some way distract you, therefore destroying your concentration and gaining an advantage. This could be done by making noises such as the rattling of coins during your swing; suddenly needing to violently cough as your are swinging; standing in your line of sight when you are putting and teeing off; or asking technical questions about your swing, stance, address, and follow through. For example, they might as you, "Why do you hold your putter that way? Doesn't it cause you to pull the ball?" What they may have attempted to do is cause you to think about it, and therefore become concerned with your grip. When you are thinking about your shots, the mind is no longer visualizing. It has become active, and you have lost the Taoist balance. It is a common ploy for practitioners of gamesmanship to get you thinking about something you are doing. In other words, they are attempting to plant seeds of doubt in your mind. This is an effective way to decrease the proficiency of the average player. Gamesmanship, however, will have no effect upon the true Taoist golfer.

Here is my golden rule for a tarnished age: be fair with others, but keep after them until they are fair with you.

- Alan Alda

There is no question that golf requires extreme concentration. Therefore, golf becomes an opportunity for others to attempt to break your concentration if indeed they consider you the opposition. Some of your more combative golfers will consider anyone that they are playing with as "the opposition." When such a golfer is attempting various strategies to undermine your confidence or concentration, they are expressing a certain type of energy. That energy has to go somewhere. If you are affected by their energies, you become the recipient. If you remain unaffected, a basic Tai Chi principle tells us that said energy will go elsewhere, most likely being reflected back to the sender. The strategies that others use to undermine your game will begin to affect their own game. This is the Tai Chi way. In Tai Chi, the practitioner offers no resistance, but also does not relinquish their position. When aggressive or unwanted energy is directed toward the Tai Chi practitioner, it becomes redirected in a circular manner which returns it. The Taoist golfer might do this with mirroring. For example, if the competitor were to ask the above question about your putting grip hoping to undermine your confidence, the Taoist approach would be to respond by asking if they had experienced such a problem in their own putting. If the competitor was rattling coins, the Taoist might ask if it were a nervous habit. The Tai Chi artist never initiates aggressive energy, but such a one is greatly adept at dealing with such projections.

We cannot prevent the birds of sorrow from flying over our heads, but we can refuse to let them build their nests in our hair.

- Chinese Proverb

To the Taoist golfer, the competitive situation offers an opportunity. This is when the Taoist golfer has the opportunity to exercise the strength of concentration, and to increase that strength. It is in times of opposition that growth and improvement can most readily occur. The Taoist, therefore, welcomes opposition without resistance. The Taoist golfer understands that he or she will always strive to excel to the greatest of their ability. If this degree of excellence is adequate to prevail in a competitive situation, so be it. If it is not adequate, that is fine also. It is all dedicated to a higher art for the Taoist. Winning and losing are two sides of the same coin, with each side containing the seed of its apparent opposite. From the Taoist perspective, there cannot be victory without defeat, nor defeat without victory.

I have learned silence from the talkative; tolerance from the intolerant; and kindness from the unkind.

- Kahlil Gibran

Since golf is greatly increasing in popularity each year, all types of individuals can be found on the golf course. There is a saying that "the best way to get to know somebody quickly is to play golf with them." Not only the wonderful qualities of an individual come to the surface in a round of golf, many of their diverse qualities also become apparent. You can learn things about their sense of honesty, self respect, patience, courtesy, confidence, perseverance, dealing with adversity, temper, concentration, balance, degree of egotism, level of awareness, appreciation for nature, competitiveness, and many other character qualities. As many golfers have found, it is a great place to conduct business, hire an employee, or choose an employer. In a sense, on the golf course, many layers of pretense and facade are dismantled. If a person has a specific character flaw, it will most likely become apparent on the course. On the other hand, if a person is truly kind, honorable, forthright and balanced, that too can be discovered while golfing. Therefore golf is not only a laboratory for learning things about oneself, it is also a way to learn about oneself in relation to others. The Taoist golfer recognizes that there are all types of people on the course, and that they are functioning from various levels of awareness. The Taoist golfer is also highly capable of identifying said level of awareness.

The sage has no interest of his own, but takes the interest of the people as his own. He is kind to the kind; he is also kind to the unkind: for virtue is kind. He is faithful to the faithful; he is also faithful to the unfaithful: for virtue is faithful. In the midst of the world, the sage is shy and self-effacing. For the sake of the world he keeps his heart in a nebulous state. All the people strain their ears and eyes: the sage only smiles like an amused infant.

- Tao Teh Ching

The Taoist golfer understands the great importance of dominion while on the course. The Taoist golfer remains mentally "at cause" with regard to the relationship on the course with playing partners. This is maintained in order to avoid becoming subject to whatever their random picture of reality, and projections might be. A Taoist remains grounded and focused within their own picture, and that which they are creating. If you allow yourself to embrace or agree with the picture of reality of others, you become effected by it, rather than at cause. Said picture then becomes an aspect of your own picture, and thus you begin to create it within your circumstances. Any information that you've acknowledged and agreed with, accepted and allowed as " the way it is" becomes *your* story. It becomes an integrated element of your reality. So the Taoist becomes like a warrior, completely conscious, awake and aware of the mental arrows unconsciously projected by fellow golfers, carefully discerning which pictures, thought forms and assumptions with which to disassociate. Discernment is a huge key to success on the course of golf, and the course of life in general. You must be the artistic creator of your own reality, rather than allowing the random projections of others to define your process and results. Everyone has a version of the way that golf is (and the way that life is). Your game will be easier if you always agree with the versions that you feel will fully enhance the quality of your game.

Your inner version of "the way that life is" becomes manifest around you. Most of your inner version may be unconscious and based upon your past experiences, and early development. Often you may not even know what it is, until it has already manifested around you. However, pictures of reality which are not engaged or emphasized cannot manifest. Your interests, fascinations and that which you deem to be important will manifest. Therefore, take dominion of your picture of reality. Write out your vision of how you want your game of golf to be. Write the highest vision/version that your are willing to accept for yourself and therefore engage. Allow yourself to be someone who golfs magnificently, naturally, with ease and grace. As you write this, it begins to integrate and become part of your story. The more you engage your conscious vision and emphasize it, the more it will become your way of life.

Who you choose to play golf with can have a significant influence on your game until you develop the qualities of a Taoist golfer. To the Taoist golfer, it makes less difference who the playing partners are because the center of awareness and attention originates from deep within their own being. The Taoist golfer will develop a sense of objective non-effect with regard to whom he or she is playing with. This non-effect is based upon awareness. It is based upon the ability to observe acutely and identify the origin of things and that which motivates others. The Taoist golfer takes nothing that a playing partner does or says personally, and always looks beyond the surface to the cause and the level of awareness. To accurately do this, the Taoist is not only aware of his or her own level of awareness at any given moment, they are also masterfully aware of what the vibrational levels of awareness are. They are aware of the fact that these levels not only exist in golf, but within all aspects of life. The golf course is simply the place where these levels often rise to the surface for easy observation, and therefore education with regard to the nature of human consciousness.

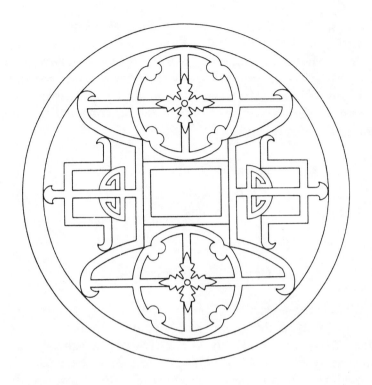

The Levels of Awareness

Taoist golfers are able to identify their own level of awareness, as well as the level of those whom they are with. It is a Taoist focus to gain inner control of the vibrational level so that they are able to remain at the highest level of awareness regardless of exterior circumstances. Objective self awareness is central to an enlightened pathway.

The following are levels of awareness which can be observed in playing partners by the Taoist golfer. These levels represent "vibrations" at which people either normally function, or vibrations that people move across, depending upon the circumstances of the moment. If good things are happening for the individual, they will go to a higher vibration. If undesirable things occur, they might go to a lower vibration. Within this system of understanding, it is the premise that each person has a basic level of awareness from which they normally function, and also all people move up an down this scale in accordance with exterior circumstances and input. The Taoist golfer has the ability to control his or her own level, and also positively influence the level at which other golfers perform.

As much of heaven is visible

as we have eyes to see ...

- William Winter

Level 13- Psychosis:

This is the lowest level of awareness in which a functioning individual could actually appear on a golf course as a golfer. Although relatively few individuals in society exist consistently in Level 13 -Psychosis, some do and are probably confined to institutions. Almost everyone, however, has visited this lowest state when circumstances trigger or evoke particular responses. Uncontrolled anger is a type of temporary psychosis, wherein one loses awareness of oneself and all others. While in psychosis, a golfer will simply swing (or flail at the ball) without any concentration or awareness. They will have fits of temper, and will totally disregard the harmony of the environment. They will be unaware of how or if they are having any effect on their fellow golfers. Such antics as the wrapping of a golf club around a tree, or hurling one into a lake, are reflective of visits into this level of awareness. It is the total loss of oneself into the realm of negative emotion, attitude or fixation. Overcoming this level of behavior on the course can easily be done with objective self awareness. The light of consciousness disperses the darkness of illusion. By becoming aware of one's own moments of psychosis, and consciously reversing that trend, said psychosis is transcended. The greater the focus of conscious awareness, the more complete the transcendence becomes. One who is in this level is perhaps the antithesis of the Taoist golfer.

Anger makes a person forget this world, the
next worlds, other people, and themself.

- Zen Proverb

Level 12 - Fear:

"That which you fear you attract." Golfers who are functioning from fear are perpetuating their own misery. To fear something is to empower it, and to suggest that the object of your fear is somehow greater than you are, and that you can be defeated by it. So fear is a type of prior submission to exterior circumstances. Those who are in fear become either tentative or desperate. Their actions often reflect an overcompensation for an intrinsic feeling of inadequacy. It is indeed that over compensation which causes the predictable failure. Overcompensation is the imbalanced Yang response to fear which is imbalanced Yin. Failure is the predictable result to any endeavor which is entered into with fear. If the golfer fears water hazards, sand traps, narrow fairways, excessive trees, deep rough, undulating greens, downhill putts, shots into the wind, or whatever it is, that aspect of the game will defeat said golfer. Overcoming fear is an immense and immediate way to improve one's game. Your consciousness has the power to transform your fears into trust. Trust is what results when you have demonstrated to yourself that you are able to master fear without need for overcompensation or aggression. This is done by confronting those fears repeatedly with awareness and patience until the monsters and demons are reduced to puppy dogs and kittens. You will then discover that what was once your greatest nemesis can become your greatest strength.

What a pity! A person lost at the crossroads of
Karma though right in the midst of paradise.

- Zen Proverb

Level 11 - Exterior Dogma

The next level of awareness is exterior dogma. Although it is two steps up from psychosis, and one above fear, level 11 remains deeply mired in illusion, and limited awareness. Here we find the one who bases all of their action upon what they feel is expected from others, or what they believe others will consider to be appropriate. It is the basic lack of trust in one's potential, ability, experiences and worth. It is the subordination of inner strength and power onto the exterior, authority figures, and society.

Although you can learn from others, no one outside of yourself can function for you. When you are exclusively motivated by those around you, you have lost your center, your Dantien. When you have lost your center, it becomes impossible to function in a conscious manner. You become like a puppet being pulled this way and that, by the expectations of others or by what you imagine those expectations to be. On the golf course, you find yourself asking for tips and instruction from your fellow golfers regardless of their level of proficiency. You become tense over your shots with worry about your performance and how it might appear to others. This level is the level of egoic self consciousness, usage of facade and inauthenticity. The golfer who is functioning in this level will usually play much better when golfing alone, or hit better shots on the driving range when no one is watching.

The Taoist golfer will of course consult experts, especially with regard to the technical aspect of their game. However, the Taoist will neither reject nor accept any input until it has been tested within the laboratory of his or her own direct experience. Once such a golfer has directly experienced the truth of any input, it then becomes their own. Prior to that, it is dealt with in a scientific and hypothetical manner. Further, the Taoist golfer seeks no approval from others, nor becomes personally concerned with the critique of others. All of this is irrelevant in the level from which a true Taoist functions.

Neither believe nor reject anything
because any other persons ... rejected or
believed it. Your own reason is the only oracle
given you by heaven.
- Thomas Jefferson

Taoist golfers captain their own ships. Someone who is mired in the level of exterior dogma is without a center, lacks presence, power, and awake consciousness. They are completely controlled from the exterior, not unlike an automaton whose responses are programmed, and therefore not spontaneous. To the Taoist golfer, every shot on the golf course is brand new. It is given full attention and awareness. It is never dealt with in a preprogrammed or automatic manner.

Exercise:

1. Evaluate your golf game. List any and all ways in which you feel exteriorly controlled.

2. On a separate sheet of paper, write down a list of new approaches which state how you intend to regain inner control of your golf game.

3. Burn the first list and keep the second one.

4. Repeat this process from time to time until you can think of no way in which you are not motivated from your own center of awareness.

Remember, who you are on the golf course functions as a reflection for who you are in your day to day life. By regaining control of one, it greatly assists you in the other. The Taoist golfer maintains interior control of both.

Level 10 - Egoic Self Aggrandizement

A natural reaction to the prior level of exterior control is "egomania," the thought or belief that one's own opinions, ideas and attitudes take precedence over all others. Whereas exterior dogma is imbalanced Yin, egoic self aggrandizement is imbalanced yang. It reflects a lack of humility which functions as a lid for growth. Those who are in this level believe that they have all of the answers and are not open to improvement. Their cup is already full, yet they have achieved no true level of mastery. It is a natural evolution from the prior level. No longer is the individual exteriorly controlled. Now they are out of control. Many, many never surpass this level because it is the highest level that is comfortable for the ego. Taoist golfers do not play from ego, however. They play from spirit.

Better to remain silent and be thought a fool

then to speak out and remove all doubt.

- Abraham Lincoln

True Taoist golfers are always learning, receiving inspiration, insight and knowledge from what occurs around them. But their center is always intact. They are motivated from within, and they have harnessed the power of consciousness which is the result of that deep sense of internal focus and awareness. This has nothing to do with glorification of the ego. The Taoist golfer is inherently humble and silent about his or her own achievements, and yet generous with encouragement for others. On the other hand, the golfer who is functioning from level 10 - Egoic Self Aggrandizement, tends to be reckless and prone toward making low percentage or unwise choices. Such a one is overly concerned about the show he or she is putting on, and whether or not it is impressive.

Level 9 - Over Experimentation

Mental Solutions

Once the golfer has fully discovered that the prior level of aggrandizement of the ego does not lead to success, but instead results in a chaotic loss of control (due to a lack of receptivity and awareness combined with overconfidence), they begin to search for mental solutions. They believed that they had it together after they overcame exterior control, and began to take charge of their own process. But they have discovered that although they now have more of a sense of themselves and their personal power, they now need to focus and channel that power and awareness in a positive and aware direction. They begin to seek a higher balance. This is the beginning of maturity.

This is the level of seeking answers from beyond the ego. They are seeking and developing plans, theories and ideas that will help them to improve. However, because this planning and theorizing is an active mental process, they have also imbalanced their approach to the Taoist game. As we have discussed before, the Taoist game involves a balanced, objective and visualizing mind. Level 9 - Experimentation, takes the body out of the play causing it to become Yin, and activates and makes the mind Yang. Therefore, the golfer in this level remains out of balance even though they have progressed significantly. The paradox of Level 9 is that the performance diminishes even though the level is higher. The golfer in this level will constantly be "trying something new." Sometimes it works, sometimes it doesn't, but the consistency is gone as well as the sense of confidence. It is a stepping stone, however, toward creating something great, profound and unwavering within.

Level 8 - Disillusionment

Once the individual realizes that mental solutions and theories are not the answer, they enter what is the beginning of a certain type of emptiness. They become disillusioned with their process of development, yet they do not know what to replace it with. Although this is a still higher level of awareness than those found in the prior levels, it is also a more difficult state of consciousness to deal with. It is not enjoyable, and no clear solutions are apparent. Upon entering this level, they become more desperate for change, for improvement and for growth. The old way isn't working; it has failed. Nothing better is visible on the horizon.

Again golf shows us why it is an ideal Taoist game. All golfers at one time or another enter this level. Golf is a demanding discipline to master, and it easily promotes disillusionment. The aspiring Taoist golfer progresses through and beyond it. Others desperately seek distraction from disillusionment by trying to recapture some prior way of functioning which was less conscious, more automatic, yet on a short-term basis, seems to work better and be more comfortable. This attempt to "go back" is a trap. It is contrary to growth, and it will not provide the type of excellent results that you truly desire. It is important to remember as the developing Taoist golfer, that if you have become disillusioned with your game, it is a very good sign. It is an opportunity. It is a time for letting go of the old way of doing things, and starting again with a fresh and enlightened perspective.

    Have patience with all things but first of all
with yourself.
- St. Francis de Sales

This level is the beginning of a type of personal crisis, because it is within this level that the individual considers totally giving up. It is a feeling of defeat. Although this level seems negative, it is not because what is actually being defeated is attachment to illusion, egotism, automaticity and unconsciousness. If the individual surpasses this level without giving up, they have actually, in the Taoist sense, completed a profound type of inner initiation which can lead them to an enlightened way of functioning. For the first time, they actually have the potential to begin the path of a true Taoist golfer.

Most who enter this level, which is known as the "Level of Opportunity," do not "pass beyond the door" and receive this initiation of spirit. It is too difficult. It requires remaining conscious and objective to one's self and inner process during a time which is quite joyless. The tendency for one who does not truly aspire toward an enlightened path is to find a way to get back to more familiar territory such as level 10 - Self-Aggrandizement of the Ego, or Level 11 - Exterior Control. To do this, one must actually find a way to lower their vibrational level of consciousness. Usage of drugs, alcohol, cigarettes, excessive eating, compulsive gambling, nymphomania, satoriasis and hyperactivity are just some examples of ways that people use to lower their vibrational levels to avoid dealing with the difficult initiation which is represented in this level. Many addictions stem from people's repeated attempts to avoid this level. Most people do not even know that they are in a process of evolving awareness, and therefore do not understand the benefit of confrontation with their own disillusionment. Society tells them that functioning from a state of disillusionment is socially unacceptable. There is social pressure on the individual to go back to the state which is less threatening to the egoic consciousness of social propriety. It is not realized that what social propriety promotes is reflected in the much lower state of awareness which is Level 11 - Exterior Dogma.

The developing Taoist understands this process. The developing Taoist knows that the level of disillusionment is a unique time of opportunity. It is the beginning of an inner initiation of spirit. If the individual does make it beyond this point of disillusionment, they will then progress into a state of awareness that few allow themselves to approach: the state of catharsis, true change. For most, this is the unexplored frontier of consciousness. Because few consciously have gone there before, it represents the unknown. And the unknown is frightening to one who has not embraced their center of power and inner awareness. But a true Taoist must embrace a pioneering spirit when it comes to the quest for the holy grail. The true Taoist knows that said grail is within.

Level 7 - Catharsis

The Catharsis Level is the crisis of being. It is a time of ultimate confrontation with one's own limitations, illusions, negativity, ego, and all aspects of oneself which are self-defeating, destructive and the causes for illusion and failure. It is the height of emotion, panic, sorrow, fear, anxiety, anger, and any emotion that has been contained within the individual psyche which is not of the light. For one who is truly intent upon excellence and mastery, the game of golf can certainly bring such emotions to the surface for the purpose of clearing them out of the psyche.

We inherit the violence of our ancestors as negative traits, emotions, fears and illusions which have been stored within the genetic code of our beings since the beginning of human existence upon planet earth. When we enter this level, we are not only clearing our psyche of negatives that have accumulated through this specific lifetime, we are clearing those which were inherited from the entire lineage of our ancestry as passed down through our genes.

This level can be described as sunlight shining over a well. The first thing that happens when light shines into a well is that all of the crawling creatures of the night retreat out of the well and away from the light. In the same way, before the waters of spirit can become pure, all of the darkness thriving "creepy crawlies" of the human psyche must rise to the surface and be cleared out. The sunlight is consciousness and the well is your psyche. The level of catharsis occurs when the intensity of your awareness has been allowed to evolve to the point in which the light of your awareness is cast upon all limitations. Among most, the tendency is to hide and distract oneself from limitations and the dark side of our nature and attempt to conceal it from ourselves and others, to pretend that it is non-existent. The level of catharsis has to do with an honest, profound and objective self-examination which involves no judgment. Simply seeing. The seeing is consciousness. It is light. The light of consciousness disperses the darkness of negativity. Self-judgment reinforces the darkness. For it, in itself, is also dark. Only the light of consciousness and objective awareness moves us through and into the next level.

> *Before you can fully see the nature*
> *and miracle of the universe,*
> *you must be able to see yourself.*

Level 6 - Detachment from Ego

Detachment is the level which is considered to be at the center of the transformation from asleep to enlightened Taoist consciousness. It is the natural result which follows the Level 6- Catharsis. It is the "emptying of the cup, so that there is room for something new, something greater." You are that cup, that holy grail.

Many people who have had near death experiences, have had "their entire life flash before their eyes." What they have actually experienced, from the Taoist perspective, is the beginning of this Level 6 - Detachment. This level actually has three phases. It encompasses the Taoist trinity of Yin, Yang and Tao.

Although several people have reported this experience of "their life flashing by" after the time of near death, physical death is not a prerequisite for embodying or going beyond this level. What it really is, is the death of egoic separateness, illusion and suffering. This level, in a sense, can be seen from the Taoist perspective as a gateway from asleep into awake consciousness.

Learn how to discern the real from the false,
the ever fleeting from the everlasting.
Learn above all to separate
head-learning from soul wisdom.
- H. P. Blavatsky

Detachment: Yin

The initial phase of Level 6 - Detachment, is the Yin aspect of the experience. It is the objective "seeing" of one's process of growth and development from a position of conscious overview. Since this "seeing" is so detached, clear and complete when one is in this level, it is the opportunity for the psyche to fully gain the wisdom from a lifetime experience.

Detachment: Yang

The Yang aspect of this level is the transformation of the entirety of one's experience (whether those experiences be negative, positive or neutral) into objective wisdom. It is the harvesting of the fruit from the tree of your life. The Yang aspect has to do with not only fully seeing your process of development without judgment, but also gaining the lesson of life in general.

Detachment: Tao

At the center is the aspect of this level which most clearly reflects the Tao. It is pure peace. This is the functioning state of this level. It is a state of the total type of peace which comes from a deep and profound sense of what is really the birth of true understanding.

The "Tao" aspect of Level 6 is by no means the highest state of human awareness as you will see as we progress. But this is a practical state of conscious awareness when the Taoist is dealing in the world. It is practical because it is invisible. Especially in Western society, the prudent enlightened adept does not go to the marketplace (or to the country club) in a state of blissful, unbridled ecstasy. The tremendous light and energy which emits from one in such a state transforms everything in its midst. Like the analogy of sunlight over the well, it brings all of the dark qualities hidden by the social facades of others, blatantly to the surface. It is often not practical.

Level 5 - Divine Science

An individual who is functioning in this level has completed the transformation of their life experience from what the Hindus refer to as "Karma" into wisdom. They are no longer subtly transferring their awareness back and forth across the Yin and Yang aspect of the prior level, thereby processing their life experience. Level Five is entered when that process is complete, and they have come to rest at the center, the "Tao" of the prior level. That centeredness and peace acts as a doorway into this higher state which is referred to as divine science.

Divine science is the immediate understanding of the intrinsic nature of all things through one's initial linkage with universal mind. This immediate linkage is the direct result of the process of transcendence of the attachment to the lower levels of consciousness which are separate, egoic and therefore incapable of embracing the unity of all things. As mentioned earlier in this book, the human mind in its purest sense, is a terminal point for the universal viewpoint. It is a microcosm. A raindrop in the ocean. In this level, the "raindrop" begins the initial stage of its experience of itself as the "ocean."

What is mind like, I wonder. It's invisible,

and as large as the universe.

- Zen Proverb

The Levels of Enlightenment

The four highest levels of awareness (Levels Four through One), represent states of consciousness which are not usually experienced by the average human being. They are levels which express the immense potential of human consciousness on planet earth, a potential which is much greater than most people can conceive or believe to be possible. The path of Taoism naturally leads one to this potential. However, it is not a goal. Instead, it is a natural result.

Although precious few are enlightened, or have expressed enlightenment down through the ages, the true Taoist understands that enlightenment is actually humanity's natural state. It is the way of nature and the universe expressed purely through mankind. Therefore, to become enlightened is not a process of adding anything to oneself. It is not a goal. It is instead a process of releasing all that is not really basic to one's nature, gently and without judgment. It is a process of simplification, of release, of clarification, and of transcendence. Rather than aspiring toward it, it is a return to divine origin, like peeling the layers of an onion. The lower levels of awareness are the outer layers. The higher levels of awareness are the inner layers. Once the entire onion is peeled, what is left? Space. That which is infinite in all directions and is therefore reflective of the true nature of consciousness, which is also infinite.

The Taoist understands that all people are in the process of this return to their enlightened and divine origin, and that at a certain point, the individual becomes aware of themselves within this process. This acknowledgement is the beginning of awake consciousness. It is the beginning of the return to forever.

Inasmuch as the *Tao of golf* serves as a process for the quickening of this evolution of consciousness, it is indeed a sacred game. To the degree that golf allows us to become more and more aware of the workings of our consciousness, it becomes a way of accelerating the process of unfoldment into a state of super-consciousness. Golf, when practiced from the Taoist perspective, is an excellent way to "peel the onion."

The following four levels of consciousness describe what is possible to all people when they can truly realize and practice the Taoist principles. Golf, when practiced from the Taoist perspective, and all of the ancient Taoist art forms, are merely a vehicle, a practice, and a "sadhana." All forms dissolve in the infinite light that is experienced in the most intense of these levels. Practicing any particular form or endeavoring to "do" anything becomes irrelevant when one is within these highest states of awareness. There is nothing left to be done in that the ultimate has already been fulfilled. There is nowhere to go, nothing to do, and no reason to do it. It is done.

Level 4 - Divine Life

This level embodies the pure experience and celebration of the bliss of physical "beingness." It is the initial realization of the immense beauty, ecstasy, and miraculous nature of our own physical presence as it connects with the "all." What an amazing creation the physical universe is. This level is a profound experiential realization of our physical connection with this universe. It is the discovery that we are not only part of the universe, but a microcosm. It is an intimate part of us, and it is all a part of something much greater. Level Four: Divine Life is the level of awe, wonder and experiential immersion in the pure blissful appreciation of nature and life.

Level 3 - Divine Love

Level Three contains all of the attributes of the prior level and yet goes beyond it. Level Three is the opening and the enlightening of the heart. The great awakening into the ever present nature of universal love that constantly permeates the very air that we breathe, and all manifestation. It can be called love for all of creation. This blissful and immense presence of love is always all around us. It is everywhere. But it is a higher frequency of existence. For us to directly experience and perceive this love, we must also be vibrating at this very high level of awareness. To do this, we must be able to transcend all of the limiting human qualities which have been inherited and passed down through the genes of our ancestors as reflected in the lower levels of awareness. The path of Taoism is one way to reach the point where this high and transcendental frequency is attainable. At times when one approaches this level of internal awareness, the exterior practices become totally secondary, whether it be the martial arts, Chinese flower arranging or the Tao of golf.

Level 2 - Divine Light

Divine light is the level of universal inspiration. It has also been referred to as the level of divine contemplation, wherein one begins to get a true overview of the miraculous nature of the creation that they are. It is the level of the true visionary because it is the enlightening of what Eastern mysticism refers to as the opening of the "third eye." The third eye is the view from within the totality of the nature of existence. It is the seer. It is the deep and experiential perception of life's meaning and purpose beyond ideas, words, thoughts or beliefs. In this level, there is nothing to believe or disbelieve because there is a total "knowingness of being" which renders all belief systems irrelevant.

Level 1 - Unity

Here is the level of total realization. It has been referred to as Nirvana. It is the opening which is the true awakening of the immense potential of human consciousness. It can be called heaven on earth. It is bliss. It is your birthright, yet few ever approach or claim it.

Before enlightenment, chop wood and carry
water. After enlightenment,
chop wood and carry water.

- Zen Proverb

A true Taoist golfer has the necessary tools and perspective to approach and experience all of the levels of enlightenment. In one sense, entering these levels of reality is the purpose of Taoism. The Taoist perspective sees that what most people believe to be reality, as they function from one or another of the lower levels of awareness, in actuality is illusion, whereas the higher levels, from which almost none function, is actually reality. So the Taoist way is paradoxical, for when a Taoist suggests that someone "be realistic," said Taoist is in actuality suggesting that said person be outrageous, enlightened, ingenious and unlimited. To the Taoist, this is being realistic. From a popular, social conscious point of view, to be realistic is to accept limitations.

Argue for your limitations, and sure enough,
they're yours.

- Richard Bach

Many people have briefly visited these higher levels of awareness at one time or another, although they may not know how they got there or where they were. The Taoist process (such as the Tao of golf, or other art forms) is like a road map into enlightenment. A developing Taoist may initially enter these higher levels as an occasional "guest." The more times said Taoist approaches the levels of enlightenment, the more he or she will remember the pathway into them and become a more frequent visitor. A grand master will become so aware of the territory of consciousness that he or she will no longer be the visitor, but instead will be the resident of these highest levels. Such a one walks quietly in the world, carrying on with whatever humble activity seems appropriate at any given moment (playing a friendly round at Saint Andrews in Scotland, perhaps), appearing from the exterior to be quite normal, but from within there is a great expanse.

> *Thine own consciousness, shining, void, and inseparable from the great body of radiance, hath no birth, or death, and is the immutable boundless light.*
>
> *- Padmasambhava*

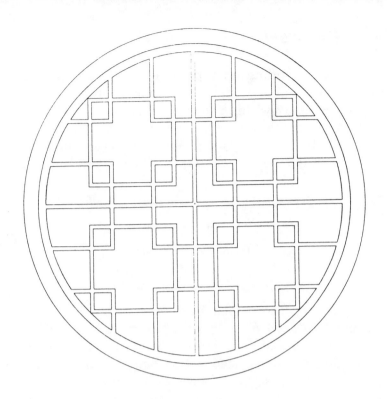

Chapter Eight

The Tao of Preparation

Your hands and feet may belong to you,

but can you always make them move

the way you want?

- Zen Proverb

The actual play which occurs on the course for the dedicated Taoist golfer can be called, "the leaves, flowers, and the fruit" of the experience. Actual play is the effect and not the cause of the optimum Taoist experience. The root, trunk and limbs of the experience of golfing (or any of the ancient and classic art forms) from the Taoist perspective, occurs within the process of enlightened preparation and practice.

By understanding how to properly prepare oneself (physically, mentally, emotionally and spiritually), mastery is much more likely within the context of any Taoist form or tradition. Remember, only "perfect practice makes perfect." This distinction is an exquisite way to describe the manner in which a Taoist golfer will approach the game.

Be careful every minute, reminding yourself,
one moment's carelessness may cause a
thousand mile difference.

- Zen Proverb

A primary Taoist focus involves the balancing of the dichotomy between discipline and relaxation. The Taoist golfer's practice and preparation routine will involve facets which exemplify both sides of this balance, understanding that both qualities are necessary. A Taoist also knows that discipline and relaxation do not contradict one another if both are present within preparation and actual play. On the other hand, discipline without relaxation becomes imbalanced Yang, and the opposite, imbalanced Yin.

The discipline aspect represents the focused precision with which the Taoist carries out the process of practice and play. The relaxation aspect is the quality which allows the practice and play to be in harmony with nature and the universe (to flow) and therefore harness the grace, power and energy that nature and the universe represent.

Suggested Methods for the Increase of Disciplined Relaxation:

One:

Stretching and Movement Exercises

With regard to stretching and movement exercises, I recommend the Arica system of psychocalisthenics as developed by Oscar Ichazo. Ichazo is the teaching master and founder of Arica (a New York based human growth movement). This is a system which integrates movement and breath while working to balance all of the muscle groups and greatly increase the potential for Chi energy flow throughout the body. From the Taoist perspective, it is one of the very finest exercise systems available. You will be amazed at the effect that this non-strenuous exercise system will have on your body after only a few weeks of daily practice. Yes, it will definitely help your golf game, but it will also improve your health and overall life experience. The Arica Psychocalisthenics System has been published by Simon and Schuster. For more information, contact the Arica Institute, 150 Fifth Avenue, #9212, New York, New York 10011. Telephone: (212) 807-9600.

 Stay loose, tight muscles are slow muscles. The Chi will be inhibited by tension.

Two:

Chi Absorption

Have a friend read the following indications for you as you do them. This is a powerful breathing exercise for the conscious increase of the Chi energy in your body. The control of breath in the body is a key to increased energy, consciousness and good health. The oxygen naturally energizes the blood, which brings life to all of the cells, tissue, and organs of the body. When the organs are functioning optimumly, the physical,emotional and mental bodies fall into profound alignment. This, (when repeated regularly), can promote results which surpass what is commonly believed to be possible for the average human. Suggestion: begin each day with this exercise:

1. Close your eyes. Become totally silent.

2. Listen for the most distant sound.

3. Imagine that your mind is an ocean.

4. Imagine that each of your thought forms are bubbles which form at the bottom of the ocean (your subconscious mind) an then slowly rise to the surface of the ocean (your conscious mind) and are then released into the air (spirit).

5. Maintain the process of watching all of your thought forms rise up and release into the air throughout this exercise.

6. Begin to breathe deeply and slowly as you imagine that your body is an immense vessel, huge enough to contain the oceans of the world and that the oceans of the world contain your breath. As you inhale, imagine yourself inhaling all of the life energy of the planet. Imagine that energy is filling up the vessel that you are, from the bottom up. The lowest part of the vessel is your Dantien at the center of your belly, followed by the middle part, which relates to your emotions, and the upper part which relates to your mind.

7. As you inhale and exhale, allow the sound of your breath to become the sound of the ocean waves as they draw back and return to the shore. Continue to see all thought forms as bubbles and release them into the air above the surface of your oceanic mind.

8. Begin to slow your breath so that the drawing in and flowing out of the waves happens much less rapidly.

9. Draw all of your breath into the lower belly region and hold it here without tension. Relax your body and gently hold the breath in the lower belly region for a count of nine. As you hold it there, imagine that the blood within your body is being greatly charged with Chi energy. As you finally release the breath, imagine that the charged blood cells are flowing to every organ in your body, enlightening and balancing them. Repeat this process just three times in the beginning because it is very powerful and should be taken slowly. Then gradually increase it. A mature Taoist will usually execute

breathing exercises with one hundred and eight repetitions. Gradually build up to this goal.

Three:

Method of the Purified Warrior

In the Yuan Dynasty, which ended in 1368 A.D., there was a legend about a remote village in Northern China. This village was in a beautiful, fertile valley and stood on the banks of a winding river. The village was blessed with great abundance, due to the fertile soil of this valley. This was by far the choicest of all the lands for hundreds of miles in every direction. Because of the great abundance enjoyed by the people of the valley, jealousy was aroused among some people of the surrounding lands. Invaders would attack the village to attempt to steal the bountiful harvest and to take over the fertile land. Amazingly, however, regardless of how vicious or battle-seasoned the invaders were, they were always defeated by the seemingly peaceful and unassuming inhabitants of this picturesque, paradise like valley. The invaders would invade and easily be conquered and the villagers would calmly return to their farming. It was from that the legend spread: The Legend of the Purified Warriors.

After the era passed when outsiders would dare to attack the amazing villagers, the attention of sages and scholars took the place of the interest of invaders. Many began to wonder what great mysteries had been uncovered by these seemingly simple farmers. What the sages discovered upon visiting the village is something which to this day, has been a well kept and time honored secret. A secret among warriors. It is the Method of the Purified Warrior.

What the villagers had discovered is that the greatest opponent in any conflict is the fear that one carries with them into battle. They discovered further that the origin of fear is actually stored within the body. They developed a method for purifying the fear from the body, thereby enabling themselves to enter any conflict fearlessly, with a clear mind, and all faculties in tact. This fearlessness and clarity gave them the necessary advantage over less enlightened aggressors: people whose motivation originated from much more mundane levels of awareness, such as greed, fear of lack, jealousy, or avarice. The villagers (from the psychological standpoint) were like mature men dealing with the pranks of unruly children. With no contest of abilities and awareness, there was no real threat of loss.

The method that was developed by the villagers was based (in a sense), on the theory of Chinese medicine itself. The villagers recognized that there are Chi energy channels which run through the body. In Chinese medicine, these are known as the acupuncture meridians. They also understood, from their experience, that fear functions to block Chi energy, thereby paralyzing the body's life energy flow and the efficiency of the overall body-mind. They also discovered that the main cause of the fear stored within the body was memory of pain. For example, if a small boy fell out of a tree and sprained his ankle, the memory of that pain would remain, manifesting itself as a fear and hesitancy, the fear being the psychological concern that the experience could be repeated at some future point. The villagers discovered that the average person's body carried a lifetime of fears, not only physical, but emotional and mental. The type of fear depended upon the corresponding painful experience memory. Also, the villagers hypothesized that there were race memories which were passed down from ancestors as fears which were inherited from prior generations.

Using the holistic theories of Chinese medicine as a foundation, the villagers developed a method of purifying and deep massage to actually cleanse the memory of fears from the body. The villagers broke the body down into psychological zones and they utilized a deep self-massage method. They did this after every battle so that their body would remain free of fear and purified. They were known throughout the Eastern world as the "Purified Warriors."

Massage Zones of the Purified Warrior

Note: The massage method of the Purified Warrior is practiced as an internal cleansing of the physical vehicle. It approaches the body with reverence, as a temple. The purpose here is to remove blockages which have been created within the body as memories of past fears. These blockages manifest themselves physically as tiny "bubbles" of fluid which have affixed themselves to the muscle system. The method of this self-massage system is to cleanse all of the muscles in the body of these tiny "bubbles." This is done with long, deep massage strokes using either the thumb or the heel of the hand. Said strokes should be administered lengthwise along the muscle fibers (not across). The massage should be as deep as possible without being painful. If the massage is painful, it becomes self defeating, because new fears are introduced into the body. You will know when you are successfully doing the method of the Purified Warrior because you can actually feel and sometimes even hear the small bubbles popping when they are cleansed. Also, there is a psychological phenomena which is quite significant. What often occurs is that simultaneous with the "popping" of the bubble, you will consciously remember the incident which originally introduced the fear into the body.

Zone One: Hands and Feet
Psychological correlation: Goals
Blockage: Fear of not Achieving Goals in Life

Zone Two: Calves and Forearms
Psychological Correlation: Means
Blockage: Inadequate Resources or Lack of Resourcefulness

Zone Three: Knees and Elbows
Psychological Correlation: Charisma
Blockage: Fear of Action

Zone Four: Upper Arms and Legs
Psychological Correlation: Capacity
Blockage: Inadequate Strength

Zone Five: Pelvic Region
Psychological Correlation: Potency
Blockage: Fear of Life

Zone Six: Abdomen
Psychological Correlation: Balance and Power
Blockage: Fear of Being Present

Zone Seven: Chest
Psychological Correlation: Impulse and Desire
Blockage: Blocked Emotional Expression

Zone Eight: Lower Back
Psychological Correlation: Support and Movement
Blockage: Lack of Adequate Support

Zone Nine: Upper Back and Shoulders
Psychological Correlation: Freedom and Responsibility
Blockage: Fear of Failure

Zone Ten: Neck and Jaw
Psychological Correlation: Determination
Blockage: Inadequate Perseverance

Zone Eleven: Mouth and Throat
Psychological Correlation: Expression
Blockage: Inability to Express

Zone Twelve: Nose
Psychological Correlation: Possibilities
Blockage: Limited Possibilities

Zone Thirteen: Eyes
Psychological Correlation: Visualization
Blockage: Lack of Perspective

Zone Fourteen: Ears
Psychological Correlation: Substance
Blockage: Fear of not Understanding

Four:

The Taoist Diet

There are seemingly endless dietary systems available
and on the market today. Usually their goals are weight
related. The goal of the Taoist diet, however, is balance. If
one maintains a balanced diet, which is free of chemicals,
excessive fats and toxins, they will approach their proper
weight as a natural result in a way which is not extreme or
temporary. The Taoist diet simply is a diet which seeks to
balance the amount of acid (Yin) and alkaline (Yang) foods
which are ingested. Toward this end, the books of Michio
Kushi are highly recommended. Kushi offers a complete
science of nutrition which is called "Macrobiotics." Those who
follow a macrobiotic diet will obtain the psysiological balance
necessary to follow the Taoist path of enlightenment. It is
impractical to assume that anyone can perform (or exist) in
a balanced way if they are not living a healthy life. The Taoist
understands that proper and balanced nutrition is basic to
good health. Further information, books, and seminars are
offered through the <u>Kushi Institute of the Berkshires</u>, Box 7,
Becket, MA 01223. Telephone: (413) 623-5741.

Five:

Awareness Putting

Perform the exercise (making use of two telephone
books for the purpose of keeping the stroke on line) in
Chapter, Five, *The Tao of Putting*, daily. If you are unable to
practice any other part of your game, practice this one. You
will be glad that you did!

Putting is a wonderful opportunity to immediately improve as a Taoist golfer. The more dependable that your stroke

becomes, the more you will enjoy the process. The usage of one hundred an eight repetitions in the Orient is a mystical number. It represents a full cycle of invocation (of calling forth a specific result). As you practice your putting each day, maintain the conscious intention that your are invoking a more and more excellent approach to the art of putting.

Putting, from the highest levels of Taoist awareness, becomes a somewhat magical experience. Personally, when I am putting from a state which approaches oneness or unity, there is a very specific and yet unexplainable phenomena which occurs. There is an actual line of light which reveals itself on the putting surface, which leads from the position of my ball to the hole, specifically following the path that the ball will need to travel.

Six:

Taoist Ball Striking

Going out to the practice range and hitting practice balls can either be an excellent and insightful experience, or a rather useless experience, depending upon one's quality of awareness.

The Taoist golfer will practice with the same focus of attention on the driving range as in a tournament or match. There is a greater challenge on the practice range to maintain focused awareness within every shot, because many more shots are hit in a condensed period of time. It is easier for the mind to wander. It is easier to become unconscious and automatic and to begin just hitting ball after ball without maintaining a relaxed discipline of consciousness. However, it is on the practice range that the psychic muscles of concentration can be greatly strengthened. If, indeed, you can stay totally in the moment, shot after shot, while hitting one hundred (or more) practice shots, it will become much easier to maintain focus while on the course itself. This is a great opportunity to improve, from the standpoint of awareness, as well as the more obvious opportunity to hone technical skills.

Exercise

While on the driving range take out your wedge. Hit as many balls as you can, maintaining total focus in the moment with no thoughts. Just observe with the mind, be active from the Dantien, and be open in the heart. If you feel that you have gotten out of the moment, or have become active in the mind with thoughts, change to the next club. Go from club to club working your way up to the driver, seeing how many shots in a row you can hit with each club from a Taoist position of balanced body, heart and mind. Try to increase the number of conscious shots with each club, and keep track of your best efforts in a small notebook.

Ideally, the Taoist golfer will hit 100 to 200 practice shots daily, if not at the driving range, then into a practice net. However, it is not the quantity of those shots that is of paramount concern. It is the quality of consciousness while taking the practice shots. For example, fifty practice shots taken with total balanced focus of awareness will be of much greater value than ten times that amount of shots hit automatically or unconsciously. Remember, all shots should be hit with correct technique. You are training your muscles and your muscles will "remember" and repeat the technique used on the practice range. If you are using a technically incorrect swing in practice, you will be training your body to permanently adapt that swing. This is why it is of utmost importance to initially have correct technical training from a PGA professional who is also in harmony with your philosophies regarding the Taoist approach to golf.

Seven:

Expansion of Taoist awareness

The following should be read to you by a friend or family member in a slow, relaxing, yet clear tone of voice. Some soft instrumental music should be playing in the background so that you can hear their voice over it. Suggested music, optimum for this exercise, would be by Kitaro, Andreas Vollenweider or Dueter. Music with lyrics, or a driving "beat" is not appropriate for this exercise. Classical selections such as Ravel's "Bolero," Rimsky Korsekov's "Scheherazade," or Bach Flute Sonatas would also be effective. Meanwhile, you should lay on your back and totally relax, breathing deeply while listening for the sound of the ocean waves within your breath. It is valuable to perform this exercise once per week, preferably at the beginning of the week (Sunday) at dawn or dusk.

Guided imagery to be read to you by a friend as you do ocean breathing:

Breathe deeply and relax totally. Allow your entire body to 'let go' and feel your relationship with gravity. Feel gravity as a warm embrace, caressing you to the planet. Allow your body to completely surrender to the embrace of the gravitational pull. Imagine that gravity is pulling any tension or stress right out of your body and into the center of the earth. Imagine that you are inhaling and exhaling universal love, with each breath that you take. Know that the love which you are inhaling and exhaling is infinite within this very moment, spanning throughout the entire creation, and permeating your body.

Imagine you are in a town high in the mountains, with one main street, a general store, a market and a post office. Smell the fragrance of pine needles from the trees surrounding the town. Imagine that you are walking down the middle of the street. There is a gentle wind blowing in your face an through your hair. Listen to the singing birds. Listen to the breathe in the fragrant air, and sense the life all around you on the quiet deserted street ... a quiet 'small town' type of energy.

The road you are walking down leads out of town. As you continue down the road, you leave the town and the road passes through pasture land, with white horses grazing there. You leave the road and decide to walk through the green, grassy pasture. There is a fence and a wooden gate. The gate is locked, but there is room for you to crawl under it and into the pasture. Feel your body rub against the moist earth and breathe in the fragrance of the slightly damp ground as you crawl under the fence. Then, getting back to your feet, begin walking through the pasture. The meadow is sunlit, and there are many flowers of all colors. Enjoy their beauty; smell their fragrance. The flowers are multi-colored, in pastels of violet and many colors of the rainbow. The wind is blowing the tall grass in an intricate tapestry of patterns.

As you pass through and beyond the meadow, you arrive at a sun-streaked forest. At the forest's edge, you come to a winding pathway which disappears into the trees. There is something that is magnetic about the pathway, attractive and almost seductive. You feel yourself almost glide onto it, and into the forest. As you walk through the trees, feel the streams of sunlight filtering through the pine needles and branches. Experience the coolness of the shade and then the warmth of the sun on your face as you proceed. Coolness ... warmth ... coolness ... warmth ... coolness ... warmth.

As you get deeper, deeper and deeper into the forest, imagine that you come to a babbling brook which runs alongside the pathway, dancing merrily over the rocks and winding through toward the deep part of the forest. Finally, you come to a wooden bridge alongside of the path. The bridge allows you to cross over the brook and onto a much narrower, winding pathway. You stop to decide which way to go and then you see a small, yet exquisite blue bird sitting on a branch across the bridge. You are naturally attracted and you cross to the other side. Here, on this side of the bridge, the trees are so tall and the branches so thick that the sunlight barely filters through at all except for a magical crystal twilight. The lighting causes everything around you to have a silver hue. The small blue bird is hopping from tree to tree down the narrow winding path as if to lure you onward, and you follow it. The bird is allowing you to come closer and closer as you continue down the path. Then, unexpectedly, it hops upon your shoulder and gently nuzzles its fuzzy little face right against your cheek. A tiny blue bird, in its own way, communicating with you. Communicating trust, peace, freedom and delicate beauty. Suddenly, the bird takes flight from your shoulder and soars around the corner of the pathway in front of you and out of sight. You follow it around the corner, and you are taken by surprise by a beautiful and magical sight.

It is an enchanted white cottage with a yellow porch. It is surrounded by a clearing in the forest, filled with carefully manicured gardens of fruit and flowers. The plums, peaches, cherries, pears, apples and melons are all much larger and brightly colored than you have ever seen. There are all kinds of flowers in every color, all in carefully manicured beds, with exquisite rock walkways throughout. The babbling brook passes through the back yard of the cottage, where there is a grassy lawn and a rock wall beyond that. As you walk up the central pathway approaching the cottage, you see curtains of lace in the windows that glisten with patterns of light which are emanating from within. You walk onto the yellow porch and there is a tiny golden bell on the door with a silver chain hanging from it. You ring the bell, and a wonderfully gentle and yet powerful voice bids you to enter.

When you enter the room, there is a magnificent sight. Sitting across from you in a huge, comfortable chair is a dazzling being whose body consists totally of light. You are drawn to that being with an open heart. As you draw closer, you see that it is you. Identical to you in every way except for the body which is totally of light. You sit across from yourself and gaze deeply into your own eyes. You are facing that part of yourself which is pure spirit. You are now able to ask one question, whatever it may be. It will be answered. Allow the answer to come.

Eight:

Profound Gratitude and Respect

Profound gratitude and respect are at the foundation of the Taoist golfer's basic attitude toward all of life. Said attitude is the only practical approach to life for the functioning Taoist because such a one truly understands the power of such an outlook. Gratitude, respect and appreciation are magnetic qualities. They are at the basis of prosperity and success. All of the universe wishes to contribute to the one who shows profound gratitude, respect and appreciation. It is a natural law. From the Taoist perspective, there is no such thing as good or bad luck. The Taoist understands that all that is attracted to the individual comes to them based upon their basic attitudes and level of awareness. No matter what occurs, whether it seems beneficial or not at the time, the Taoist will look with insight at all occurrences to find that which is there to be grateful for. To appreciate. It is a constant disposition of gratitude.

Exercise

The exercise is to begin to practice this attitude immediately. Practice it on things which you do not like, or do not agree with you. Practice gratitude and respect in times when things do not seem to be going your way. Be aware of times when you are not feeling grateful, or respectful and consciously adjust your attitude. Practice this as often as you can. Do not become frustrated in the beginning if it seems difficult to maintain this outlook. This is a new psychic muscle that you are training. It will become second nature after a short period of consistent practice of twenty one consecutive days or more.

Once you have become adept in the discipline of consistently profound gratitude and respect, you are well on your way to maturing as a Taoist golfer. The greater degree of your respect and gratitude, the greater your success and prosperity will be. The Taoist understands that this is the only practical approach to golf, and life.

Daily Routine for the Full Time Practitioner:

Mornings:

Stretching and Movement..One Hour
Chi Absorption Breathing... (work up to this)...One Half Hour
Method of the Purified Warrior.......................One Half Hour

At All Times:

The Taoist Diet
Profound Gratitude and Respect

Daily:

Taoist Ball Striking ....Two (to Three) Hours
Awareness Putting ....One Hour

Once Per Week:

Expansion of Taoist Awareness Guided Imagery

Daily Routine for the Part Time Practitioner:

Mornings:

Stretching and Movement Exercises.................One Half Hour
Chi Absorbtion Breathing.................................One Half Hour
At All Times

Taoist Diet
Gratitude and Respect

Twice Weekly:

Awareness Putting...One Hour
Taoist Ball Striking...................................One (to Two) Hours

Once Weekly:

Expansion of Taoist Awareness Guided Imagery
Method of the Purified Warrior................................One Hour

The Five Taoist Goals

**Energy. Vigor.
Lengthening the Breath.
Clearing the Mind.
Brightening One's Nature.**

8 Taoist Golfing Meditations
Based Upon the 8 Trigrams
of the I Ching

Each of the following meditations are specifically writ-
ten for the use of the Taoist golfer directly prior to a round of
golf. That is the appropriate time to select a meditation using
what is called "The Tossing of the Coins." Said meditation
will suggest an insight and a focus which can be embraced
during that particular round to maintain a high level of
Taoist awareness.

From the Taoist perspective, all things in the exterior are reflections of an interior state of consciousness. Therefore, whatever meditation that is selected for you by the throwing of the coins is considered to be the perfectly appropriate message or consideration for that moment. To the Taoist, there is no such thing as luck, chance or random occurrences. Everything that happens in the life of a Taoist is part of a flow, a process which is the reflection and "Out Picturing" of the Taoist's internal state of consciousness.

I can't believe that God

plays dice with the universe.

- Albert Einstein

Tossing of the Coins

Throwing three coins (since ancient times) has been a convenient approach for casting what is known in China as the *I Ching*, or translated into English: *The Book of Changes*. The *I Ching* is one of the Chinese classics, and contains timeless wisdom of the Orient. The following eight meditations are based upon the eight trigrams of the I Ching. Historically, prior to the use of coins, yarrow stalk was used for casting the *I Ching*. However, this process (although an aesthetically pleasing ritual) is much more time consuming, and is not necessary for our purposes here.

Directions for Tossing the Coins

Select three coins. Any three will do, as long as they have an identifiable "head" and "tail." I personally like to use three small gold coins for the pure energy value contained within the metal. However, this is not required for the purpose of this process.

Toss the three coins on a flat surface. If two or more of the coins come up heads, draw a straight line on a piece of paper (Yang). If two or more of the coins come up tails, draw a straight line with a gap in the middle of it on a piece of paper (Yin). Repeat this process three times. You will have before you three lines which represent the three coin tosses. These three lines will indicate to you which of the following meditations is appropriate for a given day.

No minded: I see things just as they are. Why

it's me, that star in the heavens.

- Zen Proverb

The Meditations

Each of the following eight meditations can either be read to you by a friend, or put on a tape for you to play back to yourself. Soft, soothing music with no lyrics should be played in the background. The suggested music list is the same as listed in the Guided Imagery Meditation in Chapter Eight, "The Tao of Preparation." When doing the meditation, it is valuable to lie down on your back and totally relax.

Meditation One

Ch'ien; the Creative, Heaven

1. Repeat the following thirty-six times:
"I am the creative. As I see it, so it is."

2. Repeat the following thirty-six times:
"My body is the link between heaven and earth."

3. Repeat the following thirty-six times:
"There is no limit to my creative power, except for those limits that I create, and I create no limits to my creativity."

Meditation Two

K'un; the Receptive, Earth

1. Repeat the following thirty-six times:
"I am open to all insights which come from within. I am here. I am now."

2. Repeat the following thirty-six times:
"My body is the link between heaven and earth."

3. Repeat the following thirty-six times:
"I am totally connected, grounded and balanced; I draw upon the energy of the earth."

Meditation Three

K'an; the Abyss, Water

1. Repeat the following thirty-six times:
"I am able to flow. I bring life to every situation."

2. Repeat the following thirty-six times:
"I am persevering. I follow through. Regardless of the obstacle or challenge, I continue steadily onward."

3. Repeat the following thirty-six times:
"I am fluid. I am free moving and relaxed."

Meditation Four

Li; the Clinging, Fire

1. Repeat the following thirty-six times.
"I am perceptive. My understanding is immediate."

2. Repeat the following thirty-six times:
"I am light. I aspire upward."

3. Repeat the following thirty-six times:
"I am illumination. I express brilliance."

Meditation Five

Chen; the Arousing, Thunder

1. Repeat the following thirty-six times:
"I am powerful. My power flows from nature."

2. Repeat the following thirty-six times:
"I am transformative. The power that flows through me is electric."

3. Repeat the following thirty-six times:
"The power of nature and I are one."

Meditation Six

Ken; Keeping still, Mountain

1. Repeat the following thirty-six times:
"Inner peace is my nature under all circumstances."

2. Repeat the following thirty-six times:
"I am the link between heaven and earth."

3. Repeat the following thirty-six times:
"My connection is solid, my perspective is broad."

Meditation Seven

Sun; the Gentle, Wind

1. Repeat the following thirty-six times:
"I flow with natural momentum."

2. Repeat the following thirty-six times:
"My influence seems gentle, yet I can transform the earth."

3. Repeat the following thirty-six times:
"I am cleansed by the wind, and my breath is as the ocean."

Meditation Eight

Tui; the Joyous, Lake

1. Repeat the following thirty-six times:
"The very movement of my body brings me joy."

2. Repeat the following thirty-six times:
"All of my activities are transformed by my inner sense of joyfulness."

3. Repeat the following thirty-six times:
"My joy continually increases and makes all that I do seem magical, and all that I do brings more joy."

A person who does everything
as it naturally goes, gets along easily
in this world and the next.

-Zen Proverb

Programming the Mind

The true Taoist understands that the activity of your mind is the basic process which defines the quality of your experiences. If you are thinking positive thoughts about your game, you will program positive results. If you are thinking positive thoughts about your life, the same will ensue.

It is therefore valuable and important to realize that you are in charge of all the results that your mind creates in your outer reality. Basic to this is the process of visualization. Each time a thought occurs to you, it is simultaneously visualized with the mind. This can be understood as a clear message to the universe about your intentions. It is like a broadcast from you, and the more "emotional charge" that your thought possesses, the more powerful your message becomes.

Many people think about (and therefore visualize) that which they do not wish to see occur. This is a negative form of programming and will bring about undesirable results. For example, a golfer on the tee might say to himself: "Now don't slice this ball into the rough." Although the mind is saying "don't", the image, and therefore the visualization is of a slice going into the rough. That becomes the program, and therefore the message to the universe and the inevitable result.

The Taoist understands the premise that states that "the entire universe rearranges itself to accommodate your picture of reality." That which you are thinking and therefore visualizing is your picture of reality. The more "emotional charge" such as desire, fear, joy, appreciation, lust, envy, greed, anger, or love that is present at the time of your thought and visualization, the more powerful the message. For example, if you merely think a random thought, but you have no real feeling about it, it is not apt to become a significant aspect of your manifestation.

Think about, and therefore "see" that which you greatly desire. Your desire will lend power to the mind's manifestation. If you want to birdie the golf hole, think only about that. Don't think about anything else. Don't think about how hard the hole might be, or about any limitation you might believe that you have. Just think "birdie." Never think something such as "don't bogey" (unless, of course, a bogey is what you desire). Also, when you get ready to address the ball, allow the mind to become silent. Let your Dantien take over.

A Day of Expectations

I truly love to play golf by myself in a slow, leisurely fashion. I love the deep sense of communion with the course, the natural surroundings, and the Tao.

I feel fortunate, because my home course in Western Washington gets most of its play in the summer months. During the rainy winter season, the course is (for the most part) only used by a small percentage of the members. Many of the members are "snow birds" who live here during the summer months, and live in places like Arizona, California, or Hawaii during the winter. Therefore, it is not at all unusual to be able to go out on the course on a sunny autumn or winter day, and play eighteen holes (or more) without even coming across another golfer. It is such a day that I wish to tell you about now. It was a day for insight and a day of expectations.

I began in my usual way by doing my morning meditation, followed by my stretching exercises. I then went to the driving range to hit a bucket of balls. My swing felt fluid and strong. I hit about two thirds of the balls. I was hitting them with consistency and accuracy, so rather than hit the remaining balls, I decided to go directly out to the first tee.

The morning sun was shining through the large Douglas fir trees that border the first hole, and its light was reflecting like endless diamonds off the puddles of standing water which remained in the fairway from the prior night's rainfall. As I stood there, three deer, a doe, and two fawns, walked slowly across the fairway and stopped just about twenty feet away. The doe bent over and began drinking from one of the puddles while the fawns went bounding after each other in a playful frolic. The wind was blowing gently in my face and whispering through the trees. There was a profound sense of the auspicious in the air.

I teed up my Slazenger golf ball and gazed down the sunlit fairway toward the area where I wished to have my tee shot land. I like to use the Slazenger because the middle three letters spell out the word "Zen." The first hole is a short par five. If the ball is hit to the right location on the fairway, it is reachable on the second shot. The main challenge of the hole is that it is narrow, with many trees, and out of bounds on each side.

I was feeling very confident because the ball was flying rather well off my clubs over at the driving range. I just knew that the ball would go right to the spot I was visualizing. I was (at that point) not really concerned with what my score might be on the hole or the round. I was feeling primarily a desire to fully immerse myself in the beauty of the day and the wonderful feeling that comes from hitting solid and accurate golf shots.

My first shot was a low drive that slowly rose as it flew down the right side of the fairway directly toward the desired landing spot. It hit the fairway just six inches inside of the right rough and rolled to a quick stop on the wet grass. It was in an ideal location for the second shot toward the green. I wandered slowly up the fairway feeling quite full. When I got to my ball, I took out my fairway wood, and stepped up to address my second shot to the green. Although I hit the shot pretty well, it did not land on the green. However, I was left with a short chip and putt for a resulting birdie.

I played the front nine of the course in a sort of a trance. I was mesmerized by the beauty and by the sheer enjoyment of just being out in the silent peace, being able to play at my own pace, with no thought to any particular goal or purpose. Simply immersing myself in the "beingness" of it all.

As I walked down the fairway of the ninth hole, just for the fun of it, I began to mentally tabulate my score. I was in the process of realizing that after parring (or even bogeying) this hole, it would be my best score ever on the front nine (which is by far more difficult than the back nine, and is also one of the more challenging nine holes in the State of Washington.) I thought to myself that this was a great opportunity for me to shoot my best score ever on my home course. I parred the hole.

I decided to stop by the Pro Shop and invite Jeff (the Assistant Pro) to join me on the back nine. I figured that if I was going for a personal best, I should have a witness. I told him about my score on the front nine, and he was more than willing to join me. Jeff is about twenty-four years old, and is a fine ball striker, who aspires to join the pro tour. He is an enjoyable playing partner and we have played several rounds together.

On the tenth hole, Jeff hit first. He hit a tremendous drive, and almost reached the green, although Number Ten is a Par Four of about 320 yards. What was equally spectacular about this shot is that there is a very tall and bushy fir tree which protects the middle and left side of the fairway. Jeff's ball was hit up the right side of the fairway and it then just gently drew in around the tree and landed softly between the two sand traps in front of the green. This was the best shot on that hole I had ever seen.

I stepped up next, and took a mighty swing. The ball careened off my club face and shot off to the abrupt left as it hooked fiercely into the deep forest beyond the rough. It was my worst shot of the day, and perhaps, the month. I stood and looked at the path of the ball in amazement at myself. I had practiced none of the Taoist principles and had swung way too hard in an egoic attempt to keep up with a professional golfer who is fifteen yeas my junior. Furthermore, rather than focusing on that particular shot, I was completely out of the moment, thinking about what a good score I was going to shoot on the back side. To say the least, I felt foolish.

As I walked into the forest to hunt for the ball, I decided that I was going to regain the sense of inner peace and focus which had led to my great score on the front nine. But in retrospect, it is clear that my very motivation for regaining that equilibrium was what was indeed throwing me off center. I was out of the moment. I was projected into some future time nine holes later when I would supposedly finish with my best score ever.

 Fanaticism consists of redoubling your efforts when you have forgotten your aim.

- George Santayana

I hit lousy shot after lousy shot. I would hook the ball into the left rough, trees, or out of bounds and then on the next shot, I would aim right to allow for the hook, and the ball would fly dead straight into the right rough or trees. On the green, I totally lost my putting stroke, and "three-putted" on repeated occasions. My chipping was equally poor. I was a totally different golfer. Jeff was diplomatic and consoling but it was clear that he was having trouble believing that I had shot as well as I had described on the front nine.

I feel that there is an angel within me
whom I am constantly shocking.

-Jean Costeau

As the miserable experience continued, my mood got darker and darker until my sole purpose for going on with the round of golf was to get the thing over with. I had transformed myself from a peaceful, nature loving spiritual practitioner who was virtually floating down the fairways, into a grouchy "hacker" who was unaware of anything but the complaints going on in my own head. And the more I complained to myself, the more I made shots to complain about. A memorable one was a sand wedge shot to the green on Number Eighteen from about seventy-five yards out. I hit the shot directly on the heel of the club. It flew over the green into the street and out of bounds. This was like an exclamation point ending a stream of illiterate babble. It was the shot that put me above fifty strokes on the back nine, worse than I had ever scored before one those nine holes.

I slinked home after the round, feeling somewhat dejected and inadequate. I felt I had let myself down and somehow regressed. Because I was in the process of writing this book at the time, I questioned whether I was truly qualified to instruct others in principles that I myself had just failed to use. I voice my self recriminations an doubts to my partner in life, Pamela. Pamela did what she almost always does. Using the sword of truth, she cut through the nonsense and simply told me that the only possible reason for the experience was to learn something from it. It was a lesson. She suggested I focus on what the insight was, and what this situation was offering me.

The obvious reason that came to my mind was that I had become goal oriented, gotten out of the moment, and had lost my Taoist equilibrium. Although this reason seemed accurate, it also seemed somewhat general and it told me nothing new. I decided to look deeper. Why did I lose my ability to perform well on the easier back nine? The second reason that came to mind was that I was probably "pressing," trying too hard, and not relaxing. This too seemed accurate, but not particularly profound. There was something I was supposed to learn from all of this. What was it?

I thought to myself: what aspect of my game needs the most improvement at this time? And the answer came. Tempo and power. When I began pressing on the back nine to match the skills and power of Jeff, I began swinging harder and hooking the ball way off line. I had lost my rhythm. What I needed to work on most was my tempo. I needed to be able to swing with more force without pulling the ball off line, and thereby get increased power and distance into my shots while maintaining accuracy.

I would never have decided to seek this improvement in my game if I had played that back nine well. I would have been satisfied. By playing poorly, I became aware of an area which could be improved. As I thought back to the front side, I realized that I was swinging easily with only about two thirds of my strength to insure that my accuracy would remain intact. It was clear that I needed to make an improvement in my swing.

I pulled out an old favorite book called <u>Power Golf</u> by Ben Hogan. This book is great because it takes you step by step through the specific mechanics of the golf swing. I realized that my flaw was that I was swinging too much from the top, and not getting enough leg drive and hip turn into my swing. I was trying to guide the ball down the fairway rather than just cutting loose and letting in fly. After reading the book and taking several notes, I went out to the driving range and applied the technical information to my swing. The power increase was significant and immediate. Amazingly, although I was hitting the ball much further, I was also hitting it straighter. There was no need to ease up as a way to maintain accuracy. It was an incorrect assumption that was hindering my game. I would never have looked for improvement if I had not experienced those dreadful nine holes of golf.

I strongly recommend the mental attitude that Pamela suggested to me. If you have a difficult round, look for the insight. What was the round telling you? Avoid becoming mired in the various reactions to the temporary difficulties. A negative reaction will compound and increase the obstructions. A positive and constructive response will dissolve difficulties and bring about insights. This is the Taoist way.

There is no such thing as a problem
without a gift in its hands.

- Richard Bach

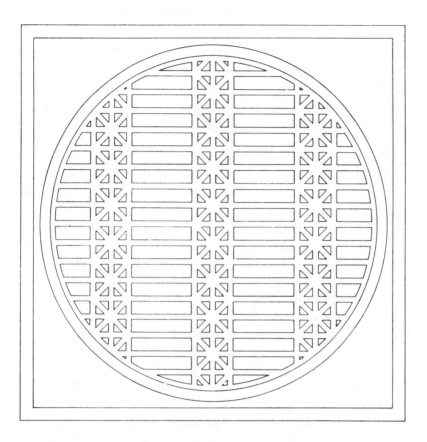

The Analogy of the Tee, Fairway, Green and Hole

    To the Taoist, it can be said that golf, and other things in life, are often viewed poetically, artistically and symbolically. Taoists see a greater inner meaning within the outer appearance of all things. The Taoist sees the profound within the mundane, the simple within the complex, and the complex within the simple. Moreover, the Taoist views all of life as a process.

    In golf, there is a wonderful opportunity for the Taoist love of poetic symbolism, The symbology in this case can be seen analogically, relating four phases of golf (the tee, the fairway, the green and the hole) to the process of human evolution. For the Taoist, human evolution is that process which leads onward toward the ultimate state of "beingness" in life, which is unity with the "all."

The Tee: Conception

From the Taoist standpoint, the tee can be seen as the opportunity to conceive, to create a new beginning. Standing ready to launch into a particular hole on a particular course, the Taoist first prepares his or her consciousness. Checking the alignment of the three centers, mental, emotional and physical, the Taoist might then visualize the exact point on the fairway to which the shot will fly. He or she will also visualize the process of the entire hole, from start to finish, while standing on the tee. The Taoist will absorb the innate feeling of joy which comes from the process of a new creation (which each hole is for the Taoist golfer). The Taoist will be focused totally in the moment.

The Fairway: Creation

After hitting the tee shot, the Taoist will approach the fairway aspect of the hole. The fairway is perceived as the process of creation. What obstacles must be avoided? Which is the best approach to the green? How is the hole to be approached? The Taoist might approach this aspect of the analogy as process, and as the unfolding of that which is being created. This is the time for versatility, creativity and strategy. But foremost, as with all aspects, what is required is the balanced functioning of the three centers. As in life and evolution, it is necessary to become more and more precise and accurate as one proceeds.

The Green: Realization

The green can be considered realization because the golfer has attained to a certain goal. The idea of being "safely on the green" basically comes from the fact that no further major hazards must be overcome. Once you are on the green, there are no sand traps to shoot over, no out of bounds, no deep roughs and no water hazards.

However, (as it is with the process of human evolution and consciousness), when one attains to a state of realization, even greater, yet more subtle amounts of accuracy and precision are necessary. When one is on the putting green, the game becomes much less physical and more a game of awareness. From the Taoist context, this is true in the process of human conscious evolution as well. Losing awareness and consciousness on the putting green can be just as costly (if not more so) than on the fairway. After all, what good is it to reach a par four hole with two spectacular shots if you follow them with four unconscious putts on the green. A two inch putt carries the same stroke value as a two hundred and seventy yard tee shot. The same focus and awareness must be applied to all shots.

The Hole: Oneness

Oneness is oneness. It is fulfillment. It is incontrovertible. Once you are inside of unity, of oneness, there is a feeling of completion, of wholeness. Yet inside of the sense of wholeness comes the feeling of a new beginning. For life is a process. Once the ball is in the hole, the Taoist will feel a sense of oneness with themselves, the course an all of life. The ball is like an extension of the self. The hole is not only an aspect of the course and the earth, it is also an aspect of the entire outer universe. It is a point in space to which the Taoist has aspired. And upon attaining that point, the Taoist moves onward, yet the experience remains within.

 If you can spend a perfectly useless afternoon
in a perfectly useless manner,
you have learned how to live.

- Lin Yutang

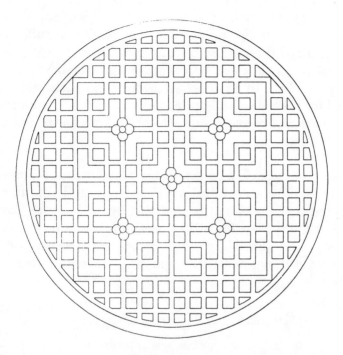

Assumption and
Intentionality

The entire universe rearranges itself
to accomodate your picture of reality.
      -Alarius

    Sometimes the most profound discoveries turn out to be the most simple. I have been writing upon this subject, *The Tao of Golf*, for a rather extensive period now. The reason for this is simple. Although I enjoy writing, I also love to golf. While other scribes may be more dutifully committed on a daily basis to their computer terminals and typewriters, I find myself spending large portions of time measuring the workings of my consciousness as it is reflected out on the golf course. Between shots, I often find myself scribbling down notes about the inner aspect of this wonderful game for later application to this book. These bits and scraps of paper have accumulated in the side pocket of my golf bag, to be pulled out later and sifted through on a rainy writing day. Occasionally, I look at one of these bits of paper and wonder "what in the heck did I mean by that?" However, no such response occurred for me today, as I pulled out my notes regarding the insight that most recently was scratched down on the back of my score card.

Today's insight is a primary one, not only as it relates to golf, but as it relates to all of life. Fully understanding, embodying and successfully applying what I wrote down today is a giant step toward mastery of the game. It will probably sound very simple and basic, but most universal truths do, yet they are all encompassing and omnipotent. It is simply this:

That which occurs in your conscious reality

is a specific reflection of your intentions

and assumptions.

On the golf course, the reality of this statement is clearly illustrated when you are putting, for example. Perhaps first, you line up the putt. Then you get a feel for the speed of the green, the grain, etc. But, do you consciously commit to the fact that it is your full and entire intention to hit the ball directly into the hole? Do you assume that it will go in? The success of your shot will reflect the power and degree of your intention and assumption. If your intention is strong, unwavering and focused, clearly you will hit a superior shot.

The power of this simple idea became exceptionally apparent to me as I was on the practice green preparing for a match with two of my regular golfing partners and the assistant pro at our club. I was putting fairly well, but I was not satisfied. I was not feeling precise about the line of the distance of the putts, and I was even missing a few easy ones.

I asked myself, "What is missing?" The following answer came from within. "Do you really fully intend and expect to make these shots?" I immediately started experimenting with the concept of intentionality. I discovered (as I experimented with it) that intentionality is an actual force that our minds can transmit. From the Taoist viewpoint, it is Yang.

Intentionality is a good word to describe an important aspect of the power of the mind. I simply started to "intend" with every fiber of my being that each putt, no matter how far I was from the hole, would go directly in. It worked better than I could have expected! The stronger my intention, the better the result. As I continued my experiment, I also noticed that doubts and fears function in the same way that intentions do. In a certain way, any doubt or fear that one might have while taking a shot (or doing anything else in life), inadvertently becomes the intention. If you doubt that you can make a shot, or fear that a shot is too difficult, you almost certainly will not make it. On the other hand, if you fully intend and expect to make a shot, you will realize a far better result.

Positive intention is like a psychic "muscle" within the mind which can be exercised repeatedly to become strong. The stronger your intention becomes, the more powerfully you will manifest your goals. A person who is able to create what they want in life, no matter what it is, has most probably discovered these laws, and have exercised and developed the mental power of intentionality and assumption.

The Tai Chi approach can be applied to psychic muscles in the same way that it applies to physical muscles. Simply stated, relaxed focus will allow optimum efficiency.

I then went out and had an exceptional round of golf with my three friends, using this power of intention as my primary focus and "swing thought" of the day. Each time I took a shot, I decided exactly where I intended for that shot to go, and the intended result. I tried to be meticulously specific about the results. This is a great key to success on the golf course. I strongly recommend it.

Have you ever noticed Paul Azinger's eyes
when he is lining up and preparing to putt?
They are filled with intention and it seems
clear that he fully assumes that it will go in.
Positive intentionality appears to utterly
emanate from every fiber of his being, and it is
quite probably grounded in his assumption
of positive results.

The Yin side of intentionality is the mysterious and perhaps even more profound force of assumption. When we assume that something is, or will be a certain way, great power is afforded toward causing the assumed effect. If you fully assume that you are a good putter, you are quite apt to putt well. If you assume that you will hit many balls out of bounds, then get ready to tally up the penalty strokes. This, of course, is not to suggest that you will be a great performer on the golf course, using only these two principles. You must first have mastered the basic fundamentals of the game. However, truly understanding intentionality and assumption is like adding fuel to the jet. It makes it really take off.

A balance between these two factors is essential. If you have negative assumptions, it does not matter how powerful your intention might be. You will be in contradiction. You might intend to hit a great shot, but if beneath that intention is an underlying assumption that you are not a good shot maker, the positive intention will then be undermined by the negative assumption. This occurs much in the same way that an unattractive background in a work of art will detract from whatever is in the foreground. It is of utmost importance to become aware of what you assume about yourself and your game. Do you assume that you are consistent or inconsistent? Do you assume that you are a bogey, a par, or a birdie golfer? Do you assume that you are a hooker or a slicer? Do you assume that you hit the ball straight? They key to mastering the art of positive intentionality and assumption is to "re-program" your mind's assumptions so that all of them clearly reflect your intentions. Believe me, this is of total importance and value to your game.

Remember that assumptions can be understood to be like a "background reality," quite like the background found in a painting. There is a background or environment, and it is from that background and/or environment that the foreground will emerge. If you have a negative, unattractive and unappealing background then the details of the foreground will also be less appealing. If you have a beautiful, positive and harmonious background, then the details of the foreground will be clear.

The idea here is to relate to your life as if it is your personal work of art, which in truth it is. Your life is your picture of reality, and it is valuable to begin with the background. To do this, you must create positive and beautiful all encompassing assumptions about your life. You must define exactly what you believe to be true about yourself now, and what you want to create for the future. To do this successfully, I recommend keeping a journal. In the first part of the journal, record a list of what you ideally choose to assume about your life, and your game. This is an ongoing list. It is not finite. This list, and vision of your life, will continue to change and evolve as you get clearer and clearer about what your intention in life truly is. It will also grow and expand as you accept greater and greater potential from yourself. Secondly, I recommend keeping (within the journal) a list of any assumptions that you discover which are counter productive to your intentions. Do not judge yourself for any negative assumptions. Simply write them down and assume, as you do so, that you are removing them from your consciousness by releasing them on the page of your journal. Then, next to this list, write down in fluorescent ink any positive assumption that you may wish to replace the negative with. This also is an ongoing and non-finite list. It will give you a history of the growth and evolution of your improving background reality. In the beginning, you will discover that your assumptions and intentions are very different from those that evolve later. Some of the negative assumptions that you have may be long term. They may have been passed down to you for generations. However, as you discover and reprogram each of these ancient primary assumptions, the quality of your life and success will take a quantum leap. Each primary or long term negative assumption that you discover within your picture of reality exists within you like treasure to be discovered. Each one that you find and release, represents a huge inflow of positive life energy an consciousness. This is, in one sense, the unleashing of the power of your universal spirit.

As your background reality becomes clearer an clearer, so too the power of your intentions will greatly grow in strength and intensity. Discipline yourself to continually alert to that which you are assuming in any given moment. If you feel things are not going your way, use it as an opportunity to examine and possibly alter your assumptions and intentions. Gaining strength in these psychic muscles is an ongoing process, but it is not arduous. It is important to not only focus, but also to relax within that focus and therefore fully enjoy the wonderful moment to moment results.

Remember, assumption is a psychic muscle just as intention is. This must be exercised repeatedly in order to gain strength and power. Once you have mastered these two principles, you will have achieved a rare secret. The secret of persevering success and pleasure. Altering intentions, however, has only temporary results. To cause ongoing and permanent improvements you must continually clarify your assumptions and alter them accordingly.

Focus, and yet relax.
And follow your spirit without hesitation.
Your spirit will constantly guide you
into wondrous joyful
and spontaneous adventures
if you listen carefully
to the small voice within.
What your spirit tells you, may
or may not make sense
to your Yang analytical mind.
But follow it anyway,
it will lead you far beyond
your self imposed limits
not only on the golf course
but anywhere, everywhere.
Golf is a great analogy for life's process.
As you keep it down
the center on the golf course,
use that as a reminder
to stay centered in
and focused upon spirit
through all of life's endeavors.
Maintain the big picture,
the universal viewpoint.
The ability to percieve
and directly experience
the vastness of all that is,
is within you.

- The Author

OTHER FINE BOOKS FROM R&E ! ! !

THE TAO OF GOLF by Leland T. Lewis. *Why do the greatest golfers all seem to play with such effortless grace?* They have mastered the Tao, or inner game of golf. The Tao is the balance of Yin and Yang, masculine and feminine, active and attractive principles that rule the Universe.

Now you can learn the mental secrets that will dramatically improve your skill and your enjoyment of the game of golf. As you master this noble game, you will discover an increased sense of inner peace and harmony and will learn to master every aspect of your life. Whether you are an occasional duffer or a seasoned pro, this book will show you the way.

$9.95   ISBN 0-88247-923-7
Soft Cover   Order #923-7

WORDS TO THE WISE: A Wonderful, Witty & Wise Collection of Good Advice on Life by Don Farias. Is life getting you down? Does it seem to be too much trouble to get out of the way of a speeding truck? Help is on the way with this collection of warm, funny and inspirational essays and poems.

You can read this book straight through, or savor it a section at a time, whenever you need a boost to get you out of bed and to motivate you to make every day better than the one before.

This book is the finest investment guide you can buy. It will help you spend your time and energy wisely so you can increase the value of your most important asset—your life. So take some words from the wise and read this book.

$6.95   LC 91-50691   ISBN 0-88247-897-4
Trade Paper   6 x 9   Order #897-4

THE DICTIONARY OF LOVE, MARRIAGE, SEX & ROMANCE by H. Gordon Havens. Marriage is nature's way of keeping us from fighting with strangers, according to "The Dictionary of Love, Marriage, Sex & Romance". This new "punabridged" lexicon of love contains quotes, wisecracks and hilarious definitions of our favorite subjects, penned by the greatest philosophers, writers and wits of the last 2,800 years. With over 5,000 definitions, this book is sure to delight and amuse both the romantic and the cynic. Buy it for someone you love.

$11.95   LC 91-50688   ISBN 0-88247-900-8
Trade Paper   6 x 9   Order #900-8

ONE WAY: Bumps and Detours on the Road to Adulthood by Jody Ewing. We all arrive at adulthood by different paths. Jody Ewing grew up on the road, traveling with her father, a champion trap shooter. Meeting other people in different parts of the country made her realize that our family, the town we grew up in and our early experiences made us the people we are today.

As a feature writer for a newspaper, she learned that there are universal experiences that we all have growing up, from the mundane to the magical.

$11.95   LC 91-50686   ISBN 0-88247-893-1
Trade paper   6 x 9   Order #894-1

UNIVERSAL KINSHIP: The Bond Between ALL Living Things by The Latham Foundation.
Here is a special book that you will want to read over and over again. This collection of inspiring and comforting articles underscores the deep bonds that unite all living things, and shows us how we all can find hope, and greater meaning as we learn to work in harmony with the earth.

Much of the *Universal Kinship* that is explored in this volume centers on the bonds between us and animals. Within the pages of this book, you will learn how pets are now attending school, not as students, but as teachers and therapists. You will discover how infants, the elderly and the sick can benefit from the presence of animals. You will also gain new insights in handling grief after the loss of a loved one. And, you will find critical new information for healing the bond with the planet we live on. This book is a must for everyone. Buy one for yourself, and for someone you love.

$22.95	ISBN 0-88247-918-0
Cloth Bound	Order #918-0
$11.95	ISBN 0-88247-917-2
Trade Paper	Order #917-2

WHAT WORKS: 5 Steps to Personal Power by William A. Courtney. Life is simple—if you know *What Works* and what doesn't. This power packed action guide is a handbook for creating your dreams. Based on time tested universal principles, this book will guide you through the five steps of personal power. Once you master these simple principles, you will be able to create anything you want, from better health, to financial success, to deeper, more loving relationships.

The principles in this book work. William Courtney used them to change his life from one of loneliness and frustration, to one of happiness and fulfillment. Now he is sharing them with you.

$7.95	ISBN 0-88247-910-5
Trade Paper	Order #910-5

YOUR ORDER

ORDER #	QTY	UNIT PRICE	TOTAL PRICE

Please rush me the following books. I want to save by ordering three books and receive FREE shipping charges. Orders under 3 books please include $2.50 shipping. CA residents add 8.25% tax.

SHIP TO:

(Please Print) Name: _____

Organization: _____

Address: _____

City/State/Zip: _____

PAYMENT METHOD

Enclosed check or money order

MasterCard   Card Expires _____   Signature _____

Visa

R & E Publishers • P.O. Box 2008 • Saratoga, CA 95070 (408) 866-6303 FAX (408) 866-0825

OTHER FINE BOOKS FROM R&E ! ! !

THE TAO OF GOLF by Leland T. Lewis. *Why do the greatest golfers all seem to play with such effortless grace?* They have mastered the Tao, or inner game of golf. The Tao is the balance of Yin and Yang, masculine and feminine, active and attractive principles that rule the Universe.

Now you can learn the mental secrets that will dramatically improve your skill and your enjoyment of the game of golf. As you master this noble game, you will discover an increased sense of inner peace and harmony and will learn to master every aspect of your life. Whether you are an occasional duffer or a seasoned pro, this book will show you the way.

$9.95   ISBN 0-88247-923-7
Soft Cover   Order #923-7

WORDS TO THE WISE: A Wonderful, Witty & Wise Collection of Good Advice on Life by Don Farias. Is life getting you down? Does it seem to be too much trouble to get out of the way of a speeding truck? Help is on the way with this collection of warm, funny and inspirational essays and poems.

You can read this book straight through, or savor it a section at a time, whenever you need a boost to get you out of bed and to motivate you to make every day better than the one before.

This book is the finest investment guide you can buy. It will help you spend your time and energy wisely so you can increase the value of your most important asset—your life. So take some words from the wise and read this book.

$6.95   LC 91-50691   ISBN 0-88247-897-4
Trade Paper   6 x 9   Order #897-4

THE DICTIONARY OF LOVE, MARRIAGE, SEX & ROMANCE by H. Gordon Havens. Marriage is nature's way of keeping us from fighting with strangers, according to "The Dictionary of Love, Marriage, Sex & Romance". This new "punabridged" lexicon of love contains quotes, wisecracks and hilarious definitions of our favorite subjects, penned by the greatest philosophers, writers and wits of the last 2,800 years. With over 5,000 definitions, this book is sure to delight and amuse both the romantic and the cynic. Buy it for someone you love.

$11.95   LC 91-50688   ISBN 0-88247-900-8
Trade Paper   6 x 9   Order #900-8

ONE WAY: Bumps and Detours on the Road to Adulthood by Jody Ewing. We all arrive at adulthood by different paths. Jody Ewing grew up on the road, traveling with her father, a champion trap shooter. Meeting other people in different parts of the country made her realize that our family, the town we grew up in and our early experiences made us the people we are today.

As a feature writer for a newspaper, she learned that there are universal experiences that we all have growing up, from the mundane to the magical.

$11.95   LC 91-50686   ISBN 0-88247-893-1
Trade paper   6 x 9   Order #894-1